CityPack
Singapore

VIVIEN LYTTON

*Vivien Lytton has lived in
Singapore and worked in
publishing, project managing
illustrated books on Southeast
Asia. She maintains a close
interest in the region, and in
Singapore – one of the world's
great crossroads – in
particular.*

City-centre
map on inside
back cover

Contents

About this book

KEY TO SYMBOLS

✛ Map reference to the location on the fold-out map accompanying this book

🚌 Nearest bus route

🖂 Address

🛳 Nearest riverboat or ferry stop

☎ Telephone number

♿ Facilities for visitors with disabilities

🕐 Opening times

✋ Admission charge

🍴 Restaurant or café on premises or nearby

↔ Other nearby places of interest

🚇 Nearest mass rapid transit (MRT/underground) station

❓ Tours, lectures or special events

🚆 Nearest railway station

➤ Indicates the page where you will find a fuller description

ℹ Tourist information

ORGANISATION

Citypack Singapore is divided into six sections to cover the six most important aspects of your visit to Singapore:

- An overview of the city and its people
- Itineraries, walks and excursions
- The Top 25 Sights to visit
- Features about different aspects of the city that make it special
- Detailed listings of restaurants, hotels, shops and nightlife
- Practical information

In addition, text boxes provide fascinating extra facts and snippets, highlights of places to visit and practical advice.

CROSS-REFERENCES

To help you make the most of your visit, cross-references, indicated by ➤, show you where to find additional information about a place or subject.

MAPS

The fold-out map in the wallet at the back of the book is a comprehensive street plan of Singapore. All map references in the book refer to this map. For example, the Sri Mariamman Temple on South Bridge Road has the following information: ✛ **bII; E8** indicating the grid square of the enlarged inset map (**bII**) and that of the main map (**E8**) in which the Temple will be found.

The Singapore Island and city-centre maps on the inside front and back covers of the book are for quick reference. They show the Top 25 Sights, described on pages 24–48, which are clearly numbered **❶ –㉕** in suggested viewing order, not page number.

ADMISSION CHARGES

An indication of the admission charge for sights is given by categorising the standard adult rate as follows: ✋ expensive (more than S$15), ✋ moderate (S$8–S$15) and ✋ inexpensive (under S$8).

SINGAPORE *life*

INTRODUCING SINGAPORE

Singapore River comes to life

After decades of being a backwater following the development of the modern port areas, ambitious projects to develop the banks of the Singapore River as eating and entertainment areas have turned the river bank into a more bustling place. The carefully restored and re-created shophouses (ground-floor shops with dwellings above) and warehouses along Boat Quay, Clarke Quay and the upper river now offer a wide selection of theme restaurants and shops that draw tourists and office workers alike (► 36, 38).

In many ways Singapore is a model city-state. It is relatively small as world capitals go, over-whelmingly modern, spotlessly clean and with few shortcomings when it comes to the fabric of the city. Singapore's many hotels, its transport and communications systems, its myriad shops and restaurants and its economic activities are diverse and impressive and seemingly Western. But if you scratch the surface you will find a very Asian city, a mosaic of Asian peoples and influences. In spite of the island's rapid development since the 1960s and despite its cityscape of tower blocks, highways and glitzy shopping centres, pockets of old Singapore can still be found. The core of old Chinatown hums with traders. Chinese opera performances can be chanced upon. Indian fortune-tellers give pavement consultations. Malay foodstalls appear at dusk near mosques in the month of Ramadan. Gin and tonic is still taken on the veranda of the Cricket Club. And a few small oases of virgin rainforest and mangrove provide welcome respite from the concrete jungle.

The almost 60 islands – nearly half inhabited – that form the republic are just over 97km north of the equator. The climate is tropical – very tropical – with average humidity above 90 per cent and the temeperature range rarely wavering from a noon high of 31°C and a night-time low of 24°C. Despite construction modern urban areas are strikingly green, with tree-lined avenues and small parks all around. Apart from some of Southeast Asia's tallest buildings and

Singapore's port handles more tonnage than any other port in the world

the occasional hill, Singapore is very flat, with little of the island above 15m. The Singapore River
still bisects the centre of the city, with the core of
the original colonial government buildings and
the Padang – the colonial 'village green' – on the
north bank and remnants of the old areas originally settled by Indians, Arab and Malay inhabitants beyond. To the south is the main business
district, with Chinatown hard on its heels to the
west. Today the mouth of the river is dwarfed by
the skyscrapers of Raffles Place and confined by
huge land reclamations to the north, east and
south. Another distinctive area is Orchard Road,
the city's premier shopping street. Here, in the
glamour of shopping mall after shopping mall,
you can buy from all over the world.

*Lion dances symbolise good
fortune*

Beyond the city core are extensive residential
and industrial areas, in particular a number of
new towns – block after block of medium- and
high-rise apartments. Originally developed as
public housing, most homes are now privately
owned. These towns are self-sufficient, with
good eating, shopping, educational and recreational amenities, and most are linked to the
centre of the city by a modern, partly underground rail system known as the MRT (mass
rapid transit). Imaginative landscaping and constant upgrading is transforming the appearance
of many estates.

The population of Singapore is predominantly
Overseas Chinese (ethnic Chinese living in
countries other than China), who form 77 per
cent of the state's inhabitants. Many arrived
only a few generations ago from provinces in
southern China and elsewhere. Malays are the
next largest sector and make up 14 per cent of
the population, Indians form 7 per cent and
Eurasians and other ethnic minorities comprise
the balance. As a result of Singapore's trading
and colonial history and importance today as a
regional hub, there are also half a million expatriate workers from all over the world.
Singapore's numerous festivals and traditions
(▶ 22) amply demonstrate its cultural diversity.

Gone shopping

Singapore is a largely affluent
and materialistic society and
shopping is a national obsession.
Retailers of exclusive clothing,
jewellery and accessories abound
and on weekends the shopping
precincts of Orchard Road, City
Hall Station and Marina Square
buzz with activity as locals and
visitors alike take to the streets
with zeal. Although Singapore is
no longer a bargain, prices for
most goods are lower than in
London, New York, Tokyo and
Sydney.

PEOPLE & EVENTS FROM HISTORY

Fast work

In just one week, Raffles made a deal with the local sultans to lease the island and appointed William Farquhar as governor. Within four months, more than 4,000 people had settled in Singapore. By the time Raffles returned in 1822, more than 3,000 vessels had registered at the port and the population had expanded to 10,000.

Japanese occupation

In 1942 the Japanese launched their attack on Singapore from Johor Bahru, at the southern tip of the Malay Peninsula, having already overrun Malaya within six weeks. Despite being outnumbered three to one, the Japanese army gained control of Singapore in just a few days, during which time tens of thousands of British, Indian and Australian troops were killed or wounded. During the Occupation up to 50,000 Chinese men were executed and the Allied troops were interned or dispatched to work on the infamous 'Death' Railway in Myanmar (formerly Burma).

FROM TEMASEK TO SINGAPURA

According to the *Malay Chronicles*, a 16th-century mixture of Hindu and Srivijayan folklore, a Palembang prince named Parameswara arrived on the island, then called Temasek, in the 13th century. He sighted a strange animal, which he described as a lion. Parameswara ousted the Malay ruler of Temasek and named his new kingdom 'Singapura', Sanskrit for 'Lion City'.

RAFFLES – FOUNDER OF SINGAPORE

Thomas Stamford Raffles (1781–1826) was the son of a sea captain. At the age of 14 he started work as a clerk in the East India Company in London. In 1805 he was appointed Assistant Secretary for Penang, then in 1811 he became Governor-Lieutenant of Java, and in 1818 Governor-Lieutenant of Bencoolen (now called Bengkulu), a port in southwest Sumatra. He soon realised that a port more advantageously located than either Penang or Bencoolen would be a great benefit to trading interests in the region, and in 1819 he landed in Singapore and secured the island as a free trade port for the British. 'It would be difficult to name a place on the face of the globe with brighter prospects or more pleasant satisfaction', he wrote. In the nine months he spent in Singapore, he drafted a constitution, set up a land registry and drew up a town plan giving each race an area in which to settle.

INDEPENDENCE – GROWING PAINS

Britain granted Singapore self-government in 1959 with full independence on the horizon. In May 1961, the prime minister of Malaya (now Malaysia) proposed a Federation of Malay States and offered Singapore membership. Singapore's lack of natural resources and land scarcity had put it in a vulnerable position and the newly elected PAP government recognised that Singapore's best chance of economic survival lay within a larger national entity. The Federation was consolidated in 1963, but Singapore was thrown out of the alliance in 1965, due in part to its opposition to policies granting preferential treatment for Malays.

CONTEMPORARY SINGAPOREANS

LEE KUAN YEW

Senior Minister Lee Kuan Yew is Singapore's most famous citizen. A lawyer by training, he is credited with transforming Singapore, almost single-handedly, from a Third World trading port to a highly developed nation – all within 35 years. He helped form the People's Action Party in 1954 and was elected prime minister at the age of 36 in 1959. Renowned for his hard work and discipline, he encouraged developments in education, housing, infrastructure and manufacturing with amazing results (albeit discouraging criticism and dissent). During his premiership the economic growth rate averaged 9 per cent per year, literacy rates rose to more than 90 per cent and today there is almost full employment. Despite stepping aside as prime minister in 1990, Lee remains active and vocal as senior minister. His advice and opinions are still sought by governments and organisations abroad.

Lee Kuan Yew (b. 1923)

CATHERINE LIM

Catherine Lim is Singapore's best-known writer overseas, since her more recent work has been published by major British publishers and her most recent novel, *The Bondmaid*, met with critical praise in Europe and America. Lim has spent much of her career wearing more than one hat. Formerly a teacher and lecturer, with a PhD in applied linguistics, she has focused on Singapore in her writing, which includes *O Singapore! Stories in Celebration*, a collection of short stories that take a humourous look at the idiosyncrasies of Singaporeans.

CLAIRE CHIANG

Claire Chiang is a woman very much in the public eye. A sociologist and noted champion of women's issues, she juggles her work as manager of the family-owned Banyan Tree Gallery with her roles as President of the Society Against Family Violence and as a nominated member of parliament (NMP). She has extensively researched the history of immigration in Singapore and has written a book documenting little-known immigrants from China.

National icon

Singapore Airlines is consistently voted one of the world's best airlines. The airline's female flight attendants, known casually as Singapore Girls, play no small part in this achievement. Attractive, well-trained and attentive, they are distinctively attired and have become such a strong symbol of the airline, and of Singapore itself, that at one time there was even a representative waxwork figure of a Singapore Girl in Madame Tussaud's in London.

A Chronology

3rd century AD	Singapore first mentioned as 'Pu luo chung' (island at the end of the peninsula) in Chinese seafaring records.
Late 13th century	Marco Polo notes a thriving city, possibly a satellite of the flourishing Sumatran Srivijayan empire (7th–14th century). It could have been Singapore, then called Temasek. *Sejarah Melayu* (Malay annals of the 16th century) note a 13th-century Singapura (Lion City).
Late 14th century	The island's ruler, Parameswara, flees to Melaka. For 400 years Singapore is all but abandoned except for visiting pirates and fishermen.
1819	Raffles selects Singapore as a trading post because of its position midway between China and India and its proximity to newly acquired British colonies.
1826	With Penang and Melaka, Singapore becomes part of the British-run Straits Settlements.
1867	Singapore is designated a Crown Colony under British rule. Thanks to its strategic location, trade in tin and plantation crops and the new steamships, Singapore rapidly becomes a hub of international trade.
1870s	Many thousands of immigrants from south China begin arriving in Singapore. They work in shipyards and rubber plantations and as small traders.
1874	The Botanic Gardens officially open on a new site at the end of Holland Road.
1887	Henry Ridley, director of the Botanic Gardens, propagates Asia's first rubber trees. Raffles Hotel opens.
1921	Japan's increasing military might causes the British to start building coastal defences.
1942	Singapore falls to the Japanese on February 15. It is renamed Syonan-to (Light of the South).

1945	British Lord Louis Mountbatten accepts the Japanese surrender on 12 September.
1954	Singapore's first elections: a legislative council is elected to advise the governor. Lee Kuan Yew helps found the People's Action Party (PAP).
1955	Legislative Assembly set up. David Marshall becomes Singapore's first chief minister.
1957	Malaya becomes independent on 31 August.
1959	PAP forms Singapore's first government. Lee Kuan Yew (▶ 9) is appointed prime minister.
1963	Singapore forms the Federation of Malaysia with Malaya, Sarawak and North Borneo.
1965	Singapore leaves the Federation on 9 August and becomes an independent republic.
1966	Singapore dollar becomes the official currency.
1967	Founder member of the Association of South-East Asian Nations (ASEAN).
1968	British military withdrawal announced and Singapore sets up its own air force and navy.
1977	1,179ha of land is reclaimed from the sea.
1981	Changi Airport opens.
1988	Mass rapid transit (MRT) system inaugurated.
1990	Lee Kuan Yew steps aside, into the specially created position of senior minister, and Goh Chok Tong becomes prime minister.
1993	In Singapore's first presidential election, former cabinet minister Ong Teng Cheong is elected.
1999	S R Nathan replaces President Ong.
2000	Singapore recovers from the Asian economic crisis.

SINGAPORE IN FIGURES

Geography and Climate
- Area: 648sq km.
- Dimensions: 42km west–east, 23km north–south.
- Annual rainfall: around 2,400mm.
- Highest peak in the middle of the island: Bukit Timah at 163m.

Population
- 1819: 500
- 1820: 5,000
- 1824: 10,000
- 1860: 80,000
- 1901: 230,000
- 1911: 312,000
- 1957: 1,470,000
- 1999: 3,217,000.

- Religions: Taoist/Buddhist 53 per cent; Muslim 15 per cent; Christian 13 per cent; Hindu 4 per cent; other/none 14 per cent.

- Population density: 4,965 people per square kilometre – one of the highest in the world.

Languages
- Official languages: English, Malay, Mandarin and Tamil.

Economy
- Population living in Housing & Development Board apartment blocks: 87 per cent.
- Per capita income in 2000: US$27,740 from US$300 in 1965.
- Visitors in 1998: 6,290,000.
- Passengers using the airport in 1998: 23,803,180.
- Singapore is the world's busiest port by tonnage, used by 400 shipping lines and handling 317 million tonnes of freight in 1998.

Distances
- Kilometres from London: 10,851km
- Kilometres from New York: 15,321km
- Kilometres from Los Angeles: 14,103km
- Kilometres from Frankfurt: 10,269km
- Kilometres from Sydney: 6,289km
- Kilometres from Hong Kong: 2,755km
- Kilometres from the equator: 100km.

SINGAPORE
how to organise your time

ITINERARIES

Many central sights are within walking distance of each other, but the heat and humidity can make even the shortest walks sticky and tiring. Don't do too much without stopping for a drink or a cool blast of air-conditioned comfort – neither is hard to find in built-up areas. Be sure to explore some of Singapore's green spaces, too.

ITINERARY ONE	**BISHAN PARK** Take a trip out to the beautifully landscaped Bishan Park, which is easily accessible by public transport.
Morning	From Stamford Road, Orchard Boulevard or Scotts Road, catch the 167 bus north to Upper Thomson Road. Ask the driver to let you off near Ang Mo Kio Avenue 1 beside Bishan Park. Walk around the park in a clockwise direction keeping to the outer path but diverting to areas of interest, such as the fishing pond and the scented garden. The park is split by Ang Mo Kio Avenue 6. Cross this to continue your walk. Stop for a mid-morning drink at the refreshments stall near the skateboarding arena. (An option here, if you are tired, is to leave the park at the Bishan Road end, turn right and catch the MRT back to the city centre from Bishan MRT station.) Follow the path all the way around, back to Ang to Kio Avenue 6. Cross the road and follow the path around to the left, as far as the café. Look out of the park to the left for the wonderful golden stupa of the nearby Buddhist temple (▶ 48), which is well worth a visit.
Lunch	Café in the park.
Afternoon	Finish your walk and leave the park where you came in. Turn left for the nearest bus stop. Catch the 167 bus, from the same side of the road as the park, south for the 10-minute ride to the start of Thomson Road (near Mount Alvernia Hospital). Cross the road to spend an hour or two in the garden centres and nurseries grouped there. Cross Thomson Road for the 20-minute bus ride back to the city centre.

ITINERARY TWO

HOLLAND VILLAGE

This district is a favourite with expatriate workers in Singapore as well as locals. The area offers low-density housing and excellent shopping and dining.

Morning

Catch the MRT west to Buona Vista.
Walk north on North Buona Vista Road.
Turn right into Holland Drive. (There is a public swimming pool here.)
At the end of Holland Drive, turn left into Holland Avenue.
Walk until you come to the left turn into Holland Road Shopping Centre.

Lunch

Any of the area's pleasant cafés or restaurants.

Afternoon

Browse in the boutiques and speciality stores around Holland Village before retracing your steps to Buona Vista MRT.

ITINERARY THREE

THE BOTANIC GARDENS & ORCHARD ROAD

An hour's stroll in these peaceful gardens is a gentle way to start the day before the rigours of shopping on Orchard Road (► 30, 70–71).

Morning

Botanic Gardens (► 29) – the main entrance is at the bottom of Cluny Road. Be sure to visit the National Orchid Garden.
Coffee at the Taman Serasi hawker centre outside the main gates.
Walk down Napier Road and turn left into Tanglin Road. Continue to Tanglin Shopping Centre (► 70).

Lunch

Go west on Orchard Road. Turn into Scotts Road. Cross to the Goodwood Park Hotel (► 82), a pricey but excellent lunch stop. The food court (► 65) in Scotts Shopping Centre basement is an inexpensive alternative.

Afternoon

Return to Orchard Road and turn left into the shopping bustle, keeping a lookout for Tangs (► 71), Ngee Ann City (► 30) and Centrepoint (► 71).

WALKS

A WALK AROUND SINGAPORE'S HISTORIC CORE

Allow a full day for this walk, with breaks for meals, or choose part of it for a shorter walk.

THE SIGHTS

- Arab Street
- Chinese shophouses
- City Hall
- Empress Place
- Raffles Place
- Victoria Concert Hall

Morning For an all-day walk, start as early as possible with coffee at Maxwell Road hawker centre. Walk down South Bridge Road to Smith Street on your left; take this street and return to South Bridge Road via Trengganu, Temple and Pagoda streets (▶ 26). Notice the renovated Chinese shophouses (ground-floor shops with dwellings above) and visit Singapore's oldest Hindu temple, the Sri Mariamman Temple (▶ 40). Cross over and take Ann Siang Hill, then turn left down Club Street. Turn right at Cross Street and left into Telok Ayer Street. Fuk Tak Ch'i Temple now houses a museum, while Far East Square and China Square are full of places to eat. Turn right down Cheang Hong Lim Street and then left at the end. Follow Cecil Street and D'Almeida Street into Raffles Place. Continue straight into Bonham Street and left into Boat Quay (▶ 36). Have lunch at one of the many restaurants there.

Cavenagh Bridge

Afternoon Walk along the riverbank until you come to Cavenagh Bridge. Cross over and pass Empress Place and the Victoria Concert Hall and Theatre. On your right is the Singapore Cricket Club (members only are admitted).

Cross over High Street and take St. Andrew's Road, passing the Supreme Court, City Hall and St. Andrew's Cathedral on your left. The Padang is on your right. After Raffles City you come to Raffles Hotel (▶ 24) – an ideal place for afternoon tea. Try Ah Teng's Bakery (▶ 69) or the Seah Street Deli (you can walk through the hotel and its shopping arcade to

*Victoria Concert Hall
and Theatre*

INFORMATION

Morning
Distance 5km
Time 3 hours
Start point Maxwell Road hawker
                centre
✚ bIII; E8
🚇 Tanjong Pagar
End point Boat Quay
✚ dI; E7
🚇 Raffles Place

Afternoon
Distance 5km
Time 3 hours
Start point Boat Quay
✚ dI; E7
🚇 Raffles Place
End point Victoria Street
✚ F6
🚇 Bugis

Evening
Distance 3km
Time 1 hour
Start and end point
                Serangoon Road
✚ E5
🚇 Bugis

reach these cafés). Continue along Beach Road.
Turn left into Arab Street, right into Baghdad
Street and left into Bussorah Street. Sultan
Mosque (➤ 45), at the end of this street, is magnificent. Facing the mosque, take the side street
to your left and then head right up Arab Street to
the intersection with Victoria Street. Wander
around a number of streets lined with old shops
selling cloth and handicrafts. You'll probably
need a break and a shower back at your hotel.

Evening Take in Little India (➤ 27), starting at
the beginning of Serangoon Road with the
market on your left and the Little India Arcade
on the right. Try side-street detours (including a
left up Buffalo Road, then a right into Race
Course Road, to find the banana-leaf restaurants,
where food is served on banana leaves (➤ 63) and
then walk to Serangoon Plaza. Walk back down
the other side of Serangoon Road, enjoying the
bustling side streets. You'll be tempted for dinner
long before you reach the start of Serangoon
Road – guaranteed.

EVENING STROLLS

Singapore is one of the world's safest cities, so take advantage of the slightly cooler evenings to have a good look around the city.

Night-time splendour of Raffles Hotel

COLONIAL SINGAPORE: RAFFLES HOTEL TO THE SINGAPORE RIVER

From the main entrance of Raffles Hotel (► 24) turn right and walk toward the Padang (► 35). On your left is the civilian war memorial. Continue down St. Andrew's Road. The rebuilt Recreation Club on your left was originally established for Eurasians, who were not allowed into the Cricket Club at the other end of the Padang. Passing St. Andrew's Cathedral, City Hall and the Supreme Court on your right, you come to the Cricket Club. Cross here and go down Parliament Lane, with Parliament House on your right and the Victoria Concert Hall and Theatre on your left. At the end you come to Empress Place, the point where Stamford Raffles (► 8) is thought to have first landed on the island. Walk downriver to Cavenagh Bridge and cross to Boat Quay (► 36), where numerous restaurants offer riverside dining.

CITY SHOPS: PERANAKAN PLACE TO TANGS DEPARTMENT STORE

From Peranakan Place, opposite the Somerset MRT, you will see John Little (Specialists' Shopping Centre) on the left as you walk down Orchard Road (► 30). Further down, just after Grange Road, is Ngee Ann City (► 30), a modern shopping complex anchored by the Japanese retail outlet Takashimaya. On the right, beyond the Heeren, Paragon and Promenade shopping centres, is Lucky Plaza – here the bargaining can be quite fierce and cries of 'copy watch, mister?' are heard often. Opposite is Wisma Atria, and at the end of this stretch are Tangs Department Store (► 71) and Orchard MRT. All along Orchard Road are ice-cream and fruit-juice stalls, in case you need sustenance, and benches where you can sit to enjoy the hustle and bustle. Most shops stay open until 9PM, but the restaurants usually stay open until at least 10PM and the coffee shops until 11PM.

ORGANISED SIGHTSEEING

For comprehensive information, contact the Singapore Tourism Board (STB). The *Singapore Official Guide*, which lists most tours, is free. The board also publishes *Singapore This Week* and *The Singapore Visitor*, also free. The main STB office is at Tourism Court.

✚ F6   ✉ Tourism Court, 1 Orchard Spring Lane   ☎ 1800 738 3778
🕐 Mon–Fri 8:30–5; Sat 8:30–1

CITY TOURS

Tours are generally half a day or a day in length, by air-conditioned long-distance bus. Various tours are available, including trips to: individual attractions such as the Singapore Zoo, Jurong BirdPark and Sentosa; city and island tours; historical tours focusing on Raffles, the colonial era, the Civic District and World War II; and shopping and horse-racing trips. The tours are generally worthwhile, although tours cost considerably more than going to the same places on your own, at your own pace.

Designed very much with tourists in mind, the Singapore Trolley Bus plies between some of the city's major attractions, such as the Botanic Gardens, Orchard Road, Clarke Quay and the colonial centre around the Padang. It also stops at major hotels and the World Trade Centre on Keppel Road. One-day tickets for unlimited travel are available.

🕐 Buses operate four times daily – 9:45am, 10:15am, 2:45pm and 3:15pm – starting at the Botanic Gardens. Tickets from STB, hotels or ☎ 339 6833. Tickets are also sold on the bus. For tours by trishaw, contact Trishaw Tours Pte Ltd ☎ 545 6311. Agree on the price before starting

RIVER & HARBOUR TRIPS

Main operators include:

Singapore River Cruises and Leisure
☎ 227 6863/336 6119   🕐 River trips 9am–10:30pm, departing from Empress Place and the middle of Boat Quay

Singapore Explorer Pte Ltd
☎ 339 6833   🕐 River trips 9am–10:30pm, departing from Clarke Quay

Eastwind Organisation ☎ 533 3432

WaterTours
☎ 533 9811   🕐 Harbour trips 10:30am, 3pm and 6:30pm, departing from Clifford Pier

Sunday trading

Tangs was established by a door-to-door salesman, C K Tang, in the 1920s. The shop moved from River Valley Road to Orchard Road in 1958. The devoutly Presbyterian family held out from opening the department store on Sundays until 1994, when the recession in the retail business and competition from the surrounding shops caused principles to lose out to profit. Many Singaporeans work on Saturday mornings, so Sunday is a favourite day for shopping.

War memorial

The war memorial commemorates the tens of thousands of civilians who died during the Japanese occupation. It is known locally as the 'Four Chopsticks', its design symbolising the four cultures of Singapore: Chinese, Malay, Indian and others. A service is held each year on 15 February – the day Singapore fell to the Japanese in 1942.

✚ F7   ✉ War Memorial Park

EXCURSIONS

Island ferries

CHANGI PRISON CHAPEL & MUSEUM
During World War II, some 85,000 civilians, Allied troops and prisoners were incarcerated. Exhibits at the Changi Prison Chapel and Museum portray the terrible conditions they endured – some for more than three years. Located in the grounds of the current prison, the chapel is a reconstruction of the small, open-air structure built by prisoners of war. Some prisoners managed to record their experiences of Changi, none more movingly than W R M Haxworth, whose sketches vividly capture his years in Changi. George Aspinall, then only 17, secretly photographed life in Changi Prison. James Clavell's *King Rat* draws heavily on the author's time in Changi, giving a powerful, and by all accounts, factual description of World War II in Singapore. Changi Village is a good place for lunch.

PULAU UBIN
Pulau Ubin is a rural idyll after Singapore. Small wooden bumboats run to the island on no particular schedule. During the ride you pass *kelong* – houses on stilts – that are home to a few fishing families. At the end of the Pulau Ubin jetty is a traditional village with original charm intact. Some old shophouses offer coffee and rent out bicycles. Cycling or walking is peaceful as there are few vehicles on the island. Any walk will take you by the old quarries; huge chunks of the island were removed to build Singapore's high rises and the causeway linking Singapore Island to Malaysia. Shaded trails through jungle and abandoned rubber plantations offer some respite from the heat and humidity.

SUNGEI BULOH NATURE RESERVE
Singapore's only wetland nature reserve covers 88ha. Carefully planned walkways allow you to explore brackish swamps, mangrove and mudflat habitats, and to observe tropical birdlife and many species of marine creatures, particularly mudskippers and crabs. Early morning and evening are the best times for viewing wildlife, with birdlife most evident before 10AM. From

September to March, the reserve is home to migratory birds from as far afield as eastern Siberia. An audio-visual show is screened in the exhibition centre five times a day at 9AM, 11AM, 1PM, 3PM and 5PM.

Stilt houses and boats on Pulau Ubin

JOHOR BAHRU

Johor Bahru (JB, as it is popularly known), the Malaysian city visible across the causeway from Singapore, is a marked contrast to the 'clean and green' Lion City. The Istana Besar (off Jal-an Tun Dr Ismail), with its beautiful gardens and Royal Museum, and the Sultan Abu Bakar Mosque (further along the same road), are worth visiting. Both were built by Sultan Abu Bakar in 1866 and 1900 respectively. Abu Bakar favoured all things English and the furniture and Victorian chinoiserie is reminiscent of what you might find in the quintessential British stately home. Foodstalls by the station and the hawker centre in the middle of town offer meals. JB is famed for its seafood and at weekends many Singaporeans cross the causeway. Favourable exchange rates have made JB big for shopping, although not everything you buy in Malaysia may be legally brought into Singapore, including pirated videos and software. Money can be changed from dollars to ringgit at banks or exchange bureaus in both JB and Singapore.

INFORMATON

Sungei Buloh Nature Reserve
Distance 24km. **Time** 1 hour
- ✉ Off Neo Tiew Crescent
- ☎ 794 1401
- ◷ Mon–Fri 7:30–7; Sat, Sun and public hols 7–7
- ⛟ Woodlands or Kranji then TIBS bus 925 to Kranji reservoir car park and walk 15–20 minutes. On Sundays the 925 goes the entire way

Johor Bahru
Distance 27km. **Time** 1 hour
- 🚌 170 from Queen Street in Singapore; go through the customs checkpoint on foot and rejoin any onward 170

Johor Bahru Royal Museum
- ✉ Jalan Tun Dr Ismail, 15 minutes' walk west of the border on the Malaysian side
- ☎ 02 07 223 0555
- ◷ Sat–Thu 9–4
- 💰 Expensive

21

WHAT'S ON

With its wealth of cultures, it is not surprising that Singapore takes all its festivals seriously. All the main religions are recognised and, in addition to the major festivals – taken as public holidays – there is a host of smaller celebrations and events year-round. Note that the dates of many festivals are linked to the lunar calendar and therefore vary slightly from year to year.

January	*River Raft Race*: All manner of rafts race on the Singapore River, plus bands, cheerleaders and food stalls, which all draw enthusiastic crowds. *Thaipusam*: This dramatic Hindu festival displays incredible feats of mind over matter; including walking on nails and piercing the flesh.
January/February	*Chinese New Year*: Singapore's biggest festival is a two-day public holiday with fireworks, stalls and dragon dances.
February	*Chingay Procession*: A huge street carnival based on a Chinese folk festival. Check out the lion dancers, acrobats, bands and floats.
April	*Singapore International Film Festival*
June	*International Dragon Boat Race*: Over 20 teams from different countries enter this longboat race, derived from an ancient festival. *Singapore Festival of Asian Performing Arts*: In odd-numbered years. *Singapore Festival of Arts*: In even-numbered years.
July	*Great Singapore Sale*: Orchard Road hosts this price-cutting month around July. The low prices highlight Singapore as a shopping destination.
August	*National Day*: 9th August. This public holiday marks Singapore's independence from the British. A parade and festivities culminate in a spectacular laser and firework display.
August/September	*Festival of the Hungry Ghosts*: Feasting and fun.
September	*Mooncake Festival*: A colourful spectacle named after the delicious mooncakes on sale.
October	*Thimithi*: Fire-walking ceremony.
October/November	*Festival of the Nine Emperor Gods*: A week of processions and street opera celebrates the nine emperor gods who are thought to visit earth, bringing good fortune, longevity and curative powers.
November	*Deepavali*: Lamps are lit and tiny white lights shine to celebrate the triumph of good over evil.
December	*Christmas*: Orchard Road lights up.

SINGAPORE's
top 25 sights

The sights are shown on the maps on the inside front cover and inside back cover, numbered **1–25** *in recommended viewing order*

1

RAFFLES HOTEL

HIGHLIGHTS

- Front façade
- Lobby
- Tiffin Room
- Bar and Billiard Room
- Singapore Sling
- Raffles Hotel Museum
- Palm Court
- Long Bar

INFORMATION

- F6
- 1 Beach Road
- 337 1886
- Two cafés, bakery, Chinese restaurant, grill, tiffin room, deli and 'fusion' restaurant
- City Hall
- 14, 16, 36, 56, 82, 100, 107, 125, 167
- Good
- Fort Canning Park (► 34), the Padang (► 35), Boat Quay (► 36)
- Free museum Daily 10–7; shopping arcade; STB office #02-34 Raffles Hotel Arcade; 8:30–7, 1800 334 1355/6

Those who are old enough to compare say the renovators tried too hard – the Long Bar, for instance, was repositioned to allow for a two-storey bar to cater to the hordes of visitors. But Raffles remains the Grand Old Lady of the East.

Legend Say 'Raffles' and you conjure up an image of the very epitome of colonial style and service. Established by the Sarkies brothers in 1887, the hotel served the traders and travellers who, after the opening of the Suez Canal in 1869, were visiting the bustling commercial hub of Singapore in growing numbers. Within just a decade of opening, the original 10-room bungalow had been expanded and the two-storey wings added. The main building, the front part, was opened in 1899. Over the years the Raffles Hotel has acquired a world-wide reputation for fine service and food, with its charming blend of classical architecture and tropical gardens. The elegant Raffles Courtyard is at the back of the main building.

Past clients Over the years guests have included Somerset Maugham, Elizabeth Taylor, Noël Coward, Michael Jackson and Rudyard Kipling. The Raffles Museum is on the second floor,

with Raffles Hotel memorabilia, a must-see for anyone nostalgic about the golden age of travel. The nearby Jubilee Hall presents a multimedia show on the hotel's history four times a day. Some 70 specialist shops adjoin the main building.

Sikh doorman at Raffles

NIGHT SAFARI

Singapore's Night Safari – a zoo that allows you to see nocturnal animals going about their 'daily' business – is the largest attraction of its kind in the world. Special lights that simulate moonlight were developed to illuminate this night zoo.

A world of animals The night safari is divided into eight 'geographical' zones that are home to the park's 110 species – more than 1,200 animals in all. You can expect to see animals from the Southeast Asian rainforests, the African savanna, the Nepalese river valley, the South American pampas and the jungles of Myanmar (Burma). As in the Singapore Zoo, the enclosures are 'open' and animals are confined by hidden walls and ditches. Five of these zones have walking tracks; others must be visited by tram.

Welcome to the jungle The best way to see the Night Safari is to take the tram journey – the tram is silent to avoid frightening the animals. A guide offers commentary as you pass through. Get off at the tram stations and follow the marked walking trails through each zone. You can rejoin the tram anytime; all follow the same route. Avoid using a flash on our camera as it disturbs the animals and fellow visitors.

The favourites Listen for the intermittent roaring of the big cats. The Leopard Trail is one of the busiest walking trails. You can see straight into the enclosure of the prowling leopards – only a plate-glass wall separates you from them. On the Mangrove Walk, fruit bats hang overhead in the gloom, and the elephants, giraffes, tigers and lions are always favourites. Be sure to catch the educational and entertaining 'Creatures of the Night' show.

HIGHLIGHTS

- 'Open' enclosures
- Leopard Trail
- Silent tram ride with commentary
- Mouse deer
- Tapirs
- Giraffes
- Lions
- Tigers
- Hippos
- Elephants
- Bats
- Walking trails

INFORMATION

- Off map to northwest
- Mandai Lake Road
- 269 3411
- Daily 7:30PM–midnight
- Restaurant
- Ang Mo Kio MRT then bus 138 or Choa Chu Kang MRT then bus 927
- Reasonable
- Expensive
- Singapore Zoo (➤ 31), Mandai Orchid Gardens (➤ 43)

The brightly lit entrance to Night Safari

3

CHINATOWN

HIGHLIGHTS

- Maxwell Road hawker centre
- Ann Siang Hill
- Chinese shophouses
- Chinese lanterns
- Trishaws

INFORMATION

- b–dl–lll; E8
- South Bridge Road and surrounding streets
- Numerous coffee shops
- Outram Park
- 2, 5, 12, 33, 51, 61, 62, 63, 81, 84, 103, 104, 124, 143, 145, 147, 166, 174, 181, 190, 197, 520, 851
- None
- Free
- Sri Mariamman Temple (➤ 40)

Lanterns hanging outside Chinese temple

One of the best times to visit Chinatown is just before Chinese New Year, when the crowded streets throb with drumbeats and colourful stalls sell everything from waxed ducks to hong bao, *red packets for giving money as presents. Chinese opera and lion dances add to the spectacle.*

Singapore's Chinatown This area covers the streets leading off South Bridge Road between Maxwell Road and the Singapore River. As a policy, conservation of the old buildings goes hand-in-hand with new development here, and though an improvement over destruction, the often rather cosmetic results and years of unsympathetic infilling have left only a few streets with the authentic atmosphere and activities of old Chinatown.

What to see Erskine Road and Ann Siang Hill exhibit some of the best efforts of preservation. Temple, Pagoda and Trengganu streets have many traditional shophouses and coffee shops. People's Park Complex, on Eu Tong Sen Street, offers a wide range of goods, some very local in character, such as Chinese herbs and good jewellery. East of South Bridge Road, along Lorong Telok and Circular Road, are some examples of nicely decaying shophouses that have yet to feel the hand of the conservationist. Telok Ayer Street, although much renovated, is also worth a visit. Thian Hock Keng Temple (the Temple of Heavenly Happiness) is the oldest and most beautiful Chinese temple in the city. After years of restoration, it now welcomes visitors again. The original temple was built in 1840 by Hokkien immigrants grateful for a safe journey. Far East Square includes Fuk Tak Ch'i, a former temple that now houses a museum dedicated to Singapore's Chinese immigrants.

LITTLE INDIA

Along Serangoon Road and the surrounding streets you can snatch all the sensations of India. Exotic aromas fill the air. Baskets overflow with spices. Stores are packed with colourful cloth. Many of these streets have not changed for decades. A perfect place to wander.

Origins of Little India In the mid-19th century, lime pits and brick kilns were set up in the area, and it is thought that these attracted Singapore's Indians, who were labourers for the most part, to Serangoon Road. The swampy grasslands here were also good for raising cattle, another traditional occupation of the Indian community.

Little India today The district remains overwhelmingly Indian, full of sari-clad and Punjabi-suited women, spice shops, jasmine-garland sellers, Hindu temples and restaurants. Architectural gems abound. Apart from the crowded, colourful streets and the tempting food emporiums, there is also the huge Zhujiao food market at the beginning of Serangoon Road; upstairs clothes and luggage are for sale. Across from the market, a little way up Serangoon Road, Komala Vilas Restaurant (▶ 63) serves wonderful *dosai* (savory pancakes) and *thali* (mixed curries) – all vegetarian – as well as delicious Indian sweets such as milk *barfi*. Walk along Serangoon Road and you will come to Sri Veeramakaliamman Temple, dedicated to the ferocious goddess Kali. Further on still is the Sri Srinivasa Perumal Temple with its magnificent 1979 *gopuram* (ornamental gateway). Take a detour to Race Course Road for a selection of Indian banana-leaf restaurants (▶ 63), notably those offering fish-head curry and a great selection of vegetable curries.

HIGHLIGHTS

- Sari shops
- Banana-leaf meals
- Fish-head curry
- Perfumed garlands
- Fortune-tellers
- Temples
- Spice shops
- Gold merchants

Ornate detail in Little India

INFORMATION

- ✚ E5
- ✉ Serangoon Road
- 🍴 Many restaurants and cafés
- 🚇 Bugis
- 🚌 8, 13, 20, 23, 26, 31, 64, 65, 66, 67, 81, 90, 97, 103, 106, 111, 125, 131, 133, 139, 142, 147, 151, 154, 865
- 💲 Free
- ↔ Kampung Glam (▶ 45)

27

5

ASIAN CIVILISATIONS MUSEUM

HIGHLIGHTS

- Chinese history timeline
- Nonya porcelain
- Red bat motifs
- Buddhist statues
- Literati gallery (Gallery 7)
- Jade collection
- Qing Dynasty porcelain
- Kang tables
- Islamic collection

INFORMATION

- E6
- 39 Armenian Street (near MPH bookshop)
- 375 2510
- Thu–Tue 9–5:30, Wed 9–9
- City Hall
- 14, 16, 36, 65, 77, 124, 133, 167, 171, 190
- None
- Inexpensive
- Fort Canning Park (➤ 34), Singapore History Museum (➤ 37)
- Free guided tours Tue–Fri 11AM, 2PM; Sat–Sun 11AM, 2PM, 3:30PM. Museum shop. Temporary exhibitions

Aimed at educating Singaporeans and tourists in the ancestral cultures of their homeland, this gem provides an introduction to the mainland Chinese, continental Indian, Islamic (West Asian) and Southeast Asian cultures.

Past and present development In 1997, the beautiful Tao Nan School, which dates from 1910, was restored to house the first phase of the Asian Civilisations Museum. Most of the objects in this building are Chinese. The second phase of development, due for completion in 2002, involves the stabilisation and conversion of the imposing Empress Place building as the museum's second wing to house non-Chinese artefacts. The project will present a fascinating, inspiring insight into Asia, its historical development and rich artistic traditions. This is one of three museums run by the National Heritage Board; the other two are the Singapore History Museum (➤ 37), a three-minute walk away, and the prestigious Singapore Art Museum (➤ 44).

Galleries In Phase I, there are 10 galleries devoted to religion, architecture, ceramics and furniture. Gallery 3, a real highlight, shows the all-pervading importance of symbolism in Chinese life. Exhibits explain the meanings of commonly seen motifs such as butterflies, pomegranates, bats and peonies, beautifully executed in a range of media. Elsewhere, you can view an extensive collection of ceramics, including exquisite imperial porcelain dating from neolithic times to the present. Gallery 7 explains the honourable, if rarefied, life of imperial scholars. Interactive screens throughout the museum give additional information on special topics.

BOTANIC GARDENS

'One of the first things that strikes a visitor is the richness and variety of the tints of the foliage…indeed, the number of different kinds is very large in comparison with that of a more temperate region.' – Sir Henry Ridley, Director, 1888–1912.

Botanical beginnings Singapore's tranquil botanic gardens are only a few minutes from frenetic Orchard Road. Here some half a million species grow in a variety of landscapes from rolling lawns to orchid gardens and tropical rainforest. Raffles established botanical gardens at the base of Government Hill (Fort Canning) in 1822, and the collection was moved to its present 53ha in 1859, at a time when tigers still roamed the area. Over the decades the gardens have been enlarged and landscaped. In 1877 one of the gardens' early directors, 'Mad' Henry Ridley (who earned his nickname for his evangelistic promotion of the rubber industry) propagated the first rubber trees in Asia, from which the earliest plantations on the Malay Peninsula were established. He is also known for developing a way to tap latex that did not kill the tree. Descendants of those first trees, native to Brazil, are still found in the gardens. In the 1960s the gardens supplied many of the seedlings for roadsides and parks all over the island, and the greening of Singapore began.

Attractions There is an extensive collection of orchids and many members of the diverse and useful palm family, including coconut, sago and lontar. The gardens are popular with locals, who jog, picnic and attend the frequent open-air concerts in Palm Valley. Attractions include the National Orchid Garden, the visitor centre, a cool house for high-altitude orchids, spice gardens and an eco-lake.

HIGHLIGHTS

- Rubber trees
- Bandstand
- *Cyrtostachys renda* (sealing-wax palm)
- National Orchid Garden
- Jungle Walk
- Palm Valley
- *Myristica fragans* (nutmeg tree)
- *Cinnamomum zeylanicum* (cinnamon tree)
- Topiary
- Bamboos
- Herbarium

INFORMATION

- ✚ A5
- ✉ Junction of Cluny and Holland roads
- ☎ 474 1165
- 🕐 Mon–Fri 4AM–11:30PM; Sat, Sun and public hols 4AM–midnight
- 🍴 Visitor centre restaurant and café; vending machine; hawker centre outside main gates
- 🚇 MRT to Orchard then SBS bus 7, 106, 123 or 174
- 🚌 As above, plus 75, 105
- ♿ Good
- 💲 Botanic Gardens free, admission to Orchid Garden inexpensive
- ↔ Orchard Road (➤ 30, 70–1)
- ❓ Outdoor concerts; leaflets available from the visitor centre

29

ORCHARD ROAD

HIGHLIGHTS

- Specialist shops
- Exclusive designer shops
- Coffee shops
- Borders bookshop
- Books Kinokuniya
- Takashimaya
- Sushi in the basement

INFORMATION

- C5; D6; E6
- Ngee Ann City, Orchard Road
- Daily 10–9:30. Restaurants on upper floors 10AM–11PM
- Restaurants, food courts, supermarket
- Orchard
- 7, 14, 16, 65, 106, 111, 123, 167, 605
- Good
- Free
- Post office, with overseas delivery; customer service centre; SISTIC outlet; banks

One of the world's great shopping boulevards, Orchard Road is the retail heart and soul of Singapore. Day or night, a stroll from one end to the other is a pleasure, even if you don't spend a penny; it is a people-watchers' delight.

Room to move Wide sidewalks and plenty of potential coffee stops help make encountering the cosmopolitan charms of Orchard Road a pleasure. And escaping the extreme heat that this equatorial city experiences is as easy as dashing into one of the dozens of air-conditioned shopping malls that line the street. Goods from all parts of the world are on offer, including well priced electrical items, designer fashions, antiques and gifts. Inexpensive food courts are prevalent and there are any number of good restaurants. For a fine walking tour, start at Centrepoint, near Somerset Station and walk to Tanglin Mall at the western end of the street. On the way, pause near the intersection with Scotts Road to drop in at Borders bookshop, or take in a film at the nearby Lido. Shops are open until 10PM.

Ngee Ann City The most impressive of Singapore's many shopping malls, this complex is especially popular because of its wide range of supplementary services: banks, restaurants, food courts and post office and supermarket. The stylish, pricey anchor store, Takashimaya, offers departmental shopping at its best, with lovely goods and Singapore's best food hall, where sushi is a top seller. Books Kinokuniya, Southeast Asia's largest bookshop and the plethora of the top-of-the-line brand-name shops such as Chanel, Cartier and Tiffany, are additional draws. The plaza in front of the building buzzes at weekends.

SINGAPORE ZOO

Treetops Trail, a wooden walkway six metres off the ground, lets you join the gibbons and a troop of cheeky red langurs for a monkey's-eye view of a simulated rainforest. Watch the endearing langurs as they feed, groom and play with one another.

Abandoned pets Singapore's zoo, acclaimed as one of the finest in the world is also one of the youngest. Its beginnings can be traced back to the 1960s, when British forces pulled out of Singapore and left a ragbag of family pets behind. The zoo, which sprawls over 20ha, was officially opened in 1973 and is now home to more than 250 species, some endangered and rare, such as tigers, orang-utans, Komodo dragons and golden lion tamarins. Breeding programmes have been initiated for endangered species, with some success.

Polar bears and pygmy hippos Living conditions are as near as possible to those in the wild – mini-habitats bounded by naturalistic trenches, moats and rock walls. More than 2,000 animals can be seen, none more popular than the orang-utan with whom you can have breakfast or tea, consisting of a human-style meal, apparently enjoyed by the apes. Polar bears, otters and pygmy hippos can be seen close up from underwater viewing areas, and the islands constructed for the different primates provide a clear view of these generally hydrophobic creatures. The snake house is very popular with children and the tiger enclosure is always crowded. There is a great deal to see, and if you get tired, you can always jump onto the silent tram that loops around the fine landscaped grounds, or take in one of the shows designed to entertain those not content with seeing sea lions, elephants and chimpanzees doing what comes naturally.

HIGHLIGHTS

- 'Open' enclosures
- Tigers
- Pygmy hippos
- Primate islands
- Air-conditioned shelters
- Treetops Trail
- Komodo dragons
- Children's World
- Animal shows
- Tram

INFORMATION

- Off map to northwest
- Mandai Lake Road
- 269 3411. Recorded information 269 3412
- Daily 8:30–6
- Restaurants
- MRT to Ang Mo Kio then SBS bus 138, or MRT to Choa Chu Kang then TIBS 927
- SBS bus 171 to Mandai Road then cross road and take 138 or 927
- Good
- Moderate
- Mandai Orchid Gardens (▶ 43)
- Breakfast with orang-utans 9–10AM, tea 4–4:30PM (booking necessary); animal shows 2:30–3:30PM

SENTOSA ISLAND

HIGHLIGHTS

- Cable-car ride
- Underwater World
- Images of Singapore
- Butterfly Park
- Fantasy Island
- VolcanoLand
- Cinemania

INFORMATION

- ✛ Off map to south
- ✉ Sentosa Island
- ☎ Sentosa Information Centre 275 0388. Sentosa Golf Club 275 0022
- ◷ Mon–Thu 7AM–11PM; Fri–Sun, public hols 7:30AM–midnight
- 🍴 Cafés and restaurants
- 🚠 Cable car from World Trade Centre (WTC, see below) and Mount Faber
- 🚌 To reach WTC (Telok Blangah Road): 10, 30, 61, 65, 84, 93, 97, 100, 131, 143, 145, 166, 176, 855. To reach Sentosa direct: bus A from WTC bus terminal, bus C from Tiong Bahru MRT station, bus E from Orchard Road. Last bus from Sentosa: Mon–Thu 10:30PM; Fri, Sun, public hols 12:30AM
- 🚢 From WTC ferry terminal
- ♿ Few
- 💲 Expensive. Free transport on Sentosa
- ↔ Mount Faber Park (► 56)

Even in clean and tidy Singapore the perfect order of Sentosa Island is incredible. You will either love or hate the wholesome family package of attractions, but give it a day and you may well enjoy making up your mind.

Getting there A former pirate lair and British military base, this island playground now attracts more than four million visitors a year. Sentosa can be reached across a causeway or by a cable car that runs just over 1.5km from the 116-m high Mt. Faber. The station is at the World Trade Centre.

For the active Rent a canoe or windsurfer, play a round on Serapong Golf Course (weekdays only), follow the well-signed walks and bicycle routes or relax on its 3km of beaches.

Adventure Watch a volcano erupt every half-hour in VolcanoLand and visit Lost Civilizations, Asian Village or Fantasy Island, which offers 13 water rides and 32 water slides. See more than 350 tropical marine species at Underwater World (feeding times are 11:30, 2:30, 4:30), insects galore at Insect Kingdom and more than 2,500 types of lepidoptera in Butterfly Park. Audiovisuals and waxworks relate the nation's history in Images of Singapore. Sentosa's Maritime Museum is agreeably low-tech. Visit in the evening for the laser and fountain shows, and check out the spotlighted Enchanted Grove gnome garden.

JURONG BIRDPARK

Hundreds of penguins and puffins crowded together on an icy beach is an unexpected sight just a few kilometres from the equator. And don't miss the Waterfall Aviary, where tropical and subtropical bird species fly almost free.

The world's birds Jurong BirdPark is Asia-Pacific's biggest bird park – a 20-ha home to more than 8,000 birds, many from the tropics. Some six hundred species, from all over the world, are housed in aviaries and other apparently open enclosures.

Birds of a feather Not far from the entrance, penguins live in a simulated Antarctic habitat with a swimming area. The vast glass-sided tank has 30-m wide windows. The Waterfall Aviary is the most spectacular area, with 2 hectares of forest contained beneath high netting, with more than 1,200 tropical birds. The aviary also has a 30-m man-made waterfall. A monorail gives a good overview of the park, but it's well worth getting off, to see the birds close up. The Southeast Asian Birds Aviary re-creates a rainforest, complete with midday storm, and contains more than 100 species, including the colourful parrots. Jungle Jewels is a large walk-through aviary devoted to hummingbirds and other South American species. There birds of prey and parrots shows are also entertaining. When you have finished watching birds, cross the road and take a look at the reptile park.

HIGHLIGHTS

- Penguin feeding time
- Jungle Jewels
- Pelican Lake
- Monorail trip
- Waterfall Aviary
- World of Darkness
- Crowned pigeons
- Birds of paradise
- Southeast Asian hornbills and South American toucans
- Southeast Asian Birds Aviary

INFORMATION

- ✚ Off map to west
- ✉ 2 Jurong Hill
- ☎ 265 0022
- 🕐 Mon–Fri 9–6; Sat–Sun, public hols 8–6
- 🍴 McDonald's, Waterfall Kiosk, PFS Terrace Kiosk
- 🚇 MRT to Boon Lay then SBS bus 194 or 251
- ♿ Good
- 🚻 Moderate
- ↔ Singapore Science Centre (► 42), Chinese and Japanese Gardens (► 56)
- ❓ Bird shows: All-Star Show (10AM, 3PM), Birds of Prey (11AM, 4PM), Penguin Parade (10:30AM)

White-throated kingfisher

11

FORT CANNING PARK

HIGHLIGHTS

- Christian cemetery
- Keramat Iskandar Shah
- Fort's Gothic gateway
- Spice garden
- *Bougainvillaea campa*
- Battle Box (World War II bunker)

INFORMATION

- ✚ E6
- ✉ Off Canning Rise
- ☎ 332 1200
- 🕐 Daily 24 hours
- 🍴 Restaurant at Fort Canning Country Club
- 🚇 Dhoby Ghaut
- 🚌 7, 14, 16, 32, 97, 103, 124, 131, 166, 167, 171, 174, 190, 195
- ♿ None
- 💵 Free
- ↔ Singapore History Museum (► 37), Clarke Quay and Riverside Point (► 38)

This area, known during the 19th century as Government Hill, is a historic high point – quite literally. From the gold finds of the 14th-century to Stamford Raffles' house and a late-19th-century fort, this hill has witnessed many changes in the past 600 years.

Historic hill When Raffles landed in Singapore this hill was known by its Malay name of Bukit Larangan, meaning Forbidden Hill, for it was here that the Malay kings were buried. A Muslim shrine, Keramat Iskandar Shah, was also found on the site, as was Javanese gold of the 14th century, a sign of Java's wide-reaching influence at that time. With a commanding view of the harbour and settlement, it was a prime location and was quickly chosen to be the site for Government House (the governor's residence). Its slopes were given over to Raffles' experimental garden with its variety of economically useful plants, particularly spices.

Transformations The house was demolished in the mid-19th century and a fort built, named for Viscount Canning, a governor of India. The fort, too, was demolished in 1907, to make way for a reservoir; all that remains is the Gothic gateway. On the eastern side of the hill are remnants of an old Christian cemetery. The government offices at the top, built in 1926, now house the Fort Canning Centre and accommodate a professional dance troupe, exhibition space and a theatre. You can also visit the bunker where the British Malaya Command had its headquarters in World War II.

Fort Canning's gateway

THE PADANG

The word **padang** *is Malay for 'plain', and that is just what this is. Although unrelieved by trees or hills, these few hectares offer a good breathing space and act as a focal point for the colonial buildings grouped around it.*

Recreation Once the Padang directly faced the sea, but land reclamation in Marina Bay has long since changed its outlook. The Padang, which goes back to Raffles' days, has retained its use as a recreational area. Cricket and rugby matches are played – in season, of course – and while non-members may not venture into the clubs at either end of the Padang, they can stand and watch the games. St Andrew's Cathedral, behind the Padang, was completed in 1861 with Indian convict labour. City Hall, facing the Padang, has seen several historic events: the herding of Europeans onto the Padang on the morning of the Japanese occupation, and the formal surrender of the Japanese on its steps in 1945.

Nearby buildings At the southern end is the Cricket Club, with a commanding view of the Padang. The group of government buildings includes the attorney-general's chambers (resembling a small opera house), the Victoria Theatre and Concert Hall buildings, and the former Parliament House. Turning back down Connaught Drive and Esplanade Park, you will see the outline of Suntec City – a massive conference and exhibition centre – and a group of hotels built on reclaimed land, together with Marina Square Shopping Centre. At the northern end of the Padang is the Recreation Club, originally built in 1885 for Eurasians, who were excluded from the Cricket Club.

HIGHLIGHTS

- City Hall steps
- Singapore Cricket Club
- Cricket and rugby matches
- Victoria Theatre portico
- Old Parliament House
- Esplanade Walk
- St Andrew's Cathedral
- Statue of Raffles

INFORMATION

- ✚ F7
- ✉ St Andrew's Road
- City Hall
- 🚌 10, 70, 75, 82, 97, 100, 107, 125, 130, 131, 167, 196
- ♿ None
- 🎫 Free
- ↔ Raffles Hotel (➤ 24), Fort Canning Park (➤ 34), Boat Quay (➤ 36)

Westin Stamford Hotel

13

BOAT QUAY

The bundles of rattan and sacks of rice have long disappeared, as have the coolies and boatmen, but the sweep of shophouses, the thronging crowds and the odd tour operator's bumboat give an inkling of an earlier life along the Singapore River.

Early Days After decades as a sleepy backwater, Boat Quay has sprung back to life. For a century after the founding of Singapore, Bu Ye Tian, as the Chinese used to call it, was 'a place of ceaseless activity' with little wooden bumboats and sampans ferrying their cargoes of rubber and rice, cotton and rattan, sago and spices, back and forth to ships at Tanjong Pagar Docks. The riverbank was lined with shophouses, which served as combined trading offices, homes and godowns, the warehouses used for storage and sorting. Behind this area was Commercial Square, now Raffles Place, where the big international shipping and trading companies had their commercial offices.

Changes With the opening of Singapore's large container port facilities, the bumboats departed Boat Quay and the area was left to a few traders and mechanics who continued to eke out a living there. Then, in the late 1980s, Boat Quay was designated a conservation area and life was dramatically restored to the river bank. A riverside walkway was built and the shophouses were renovated.

Active once more Bars, nightclubs and restaurants now fill the area and the riverside is awash with tables and chairs for outdoor dining. Boat Quay today is lively and picturesque – a pleasant place for a meal with views across to Empress Place, and on to the impressive skyscrapers of the financial district.

SINGAPORE HISTORY MUSEUM

Stroll through the ancestral hall and bridal chamber of a fully re-created early 20th-century Peranakan house. Don't miss the museum's 3D show that presents Singapore's history through virtual sets, animation and historial film footage.

Architectural delight The Singapore History Museum building, an exquisite example of colonial architecture, began life in 1887 as the Raffles Library and Museum. It was originally intended to be twice the size, but the Colonial Office balked at the expense. The initial collection comprised 20,000 books and numerous ethnographic artefacts and natural history specimens. Permanent displays, usually with an Asian focus and supplemented by temporary exhibitions, explore the trends and developments that have shaped Singapore's history.

Exhibits Among the items in the permanent collection are Javanese gold jewellery dating from the 14th century found during excavations at nearby Fort Canning, 20 miniature dioramas depicting significant events in Singapore's history and hundreds of jade carvings. This cache of jade was given by the Aw family, who made their wealth from the famous panacea Tiger Balm. A small gallery – Rumah Baba – displays a number of beautiful pieces of porcelain, elaborate silverware, beaded embroidery, clothing, inlaid blackwood furniture and other artefacts of the culture of the Peranakan (Straits Chinese). The Children's Discovery Gallery is interactive.

Souvenirs The museum shops, one inside the museum and the other down the road on the corner of Armenian Street, sell craft items from the region, such as Peranakan household wares, and Indonesian batik scarves.

HIGHLIGHTS

- Grand entrance
- Central dome
- Javanese gold
- *Sireh* bowls
- Beaded slippers
- Jade carvings
- Opium pipes
- Porcelain
- Museum shops

INFORMATION

- E6
- 93 Stamford Road
- 375 2510
- Thu–Tue 9–5:30, Wed 9–9
- Hawker centre (open 24 hours) next to the National Library
- Dhoby Ghaut or City Hall
- 7, 14, 16, 64, 65, 97, 103, 106, 111, 124, 131, 139, 166, 167, 171, 174, 190, 501
- None
- Inexpensive
- Raffles Hotel (➤ 24), Fort Canning Park (➤ 34), Singapore Art Museum (➤ 44)
- Guided tours in English Tue–Fri 11AM, 2PM; Sat, Sun 11AM, 2PM, 3PM. Guided tours in Japanese Tue–Fri 10:30AM. Occasional talks and other activities held by Friends of the Museum

15

CLARKE QUAY & RIVERSIDE POINT

HIGHLIGHTS

- Riverfront walk
- Street stalls
- Bandstand
- River trip
- Brewerkz
- Flea market

INFORMATION

- ✚ bI; E7
- ✉ 3 River Valley Road
- ☎ 433 0152
- 🍴 Numerous
- Ⓡ Raffles Place
- ▭ SBS bus 54 from Scotts Road; 32, 195 from City Hall MRT
- ♿ Few
- 💳 Free
- ↔ Fort Canning Park (► 34), Singapore History Museum (► 37), Sri Mariamman Temple (► 40)
- ❓ *Wayang* (Chinese opera) at Gas Lamp Square on Wed and Fri evenings from 7:30–8:30

You may not be convinced that this quay lives up to the claims that it is Singapore's answer to London's Covent Garden and San Francisco's Fisherman's Wharf, but you can't deny the popularity of these five blocks of eateries and entertainment.

Regeneration Once a riverside area of old wharves and warehouses destined for refurbishment, Clarke Quay, along Singapore River, has been transformed by one of Singapore's most ambitious restoration schemes. The quay is named after Sir Andrew Clarke, governor of the Straits Settlements from 1873 to 1875. The area was covered with godowns constructed between 1860 and 1920 by European and Chinese entrepreneurs. As the story goes, the developers bulldozed the run-down neighbourhood before they could be stopped. Maybe re-creating the buildings was an easier option than restoring? Clarke Quay opened in 1993, $250 million later. Brand-new godowns, shophouses and trading posts were constructed along the riverfront and in the streets leading up to River Valley Road. A colourful junk that doubles as a restaurant is moored in the river.

Shopping and eating The entire area is given over to shops and eateries – you can buy everything from pottery and leather goods to wooden clogs, batik prints and Chinese medicines. Outdoor dining is popular, just as at Boat Quay farther downriver (► 36). A carnival atmosphere prevails year-round, with street stalls and a bandstand complete with entertainment. The Sunday flea market has become a favourite among toy collectors, although prices can be high. If you cross the Read or Ord bridges to the opposite bank, you'll find Riverside Point, with shops, a cinema, good restaurants and the Brewerkz microbrewery.

BUKIT TIMAH NATURE RESERVE

The exhilarating walk up Singapore's highest hill offers a glimpse of the majestic tropical rainforest that once dominated the island. Bukit Timah is one of the few areas left in Singapore where the natural landscape remains pristine.

Singapore rainforest The last remaining area of primary tropical rainforest in Singapore covers 166ha of Bukit Timah (Malay for 'tin hill'), which at 163m is the island's highest point. The forest has never been logged and, apart from three quarries on its borders, is virgin forest, little changed over the millennia.

Flora Trails that start at the visitor centre allow you to observe the reserve's fauna and flora. Among the highlights are the splendid dipterocarps – a family of trees almost all of which were originally found only in Malaysia – some nearly 30m tall. Lianas and rattans trail and twist though the forest, and strangler figs can be found. The latter are so called because they begin life high in the crown of trees and grow aerial roots down to the ground, gradually encircling the host tree; deprived of sunlight at its top and soil nutrients at its base, the tree eventually dies. Smaller epiphytes, with such apt names as bird's-nest fern and staghorn fern, emerge from trunks and branches looking like unkempt bushes.

Fauna Animals are more difficult to spot, except for the marauding macaques, which gather at the base of the reserve and menace for a fight if you get too close – so don't! Visit in early morning for the greatest chance of spotting wildlife. Animals you are most likely to see include squirrels, lizards and birds such as the greater racket-tailed drongo and the banded woodpecker.

HIGHLIGHTS

- Visitor centre
- Winding forest trails
- Rainforest trees
- Strangler figs
- Pitcher plants
- Ferns
- Colourful fungi
- Macaques
- Tree shrews
- Giant ants

INFORMATION

- Off map to northwest
- 177 Hindhede Drive
- 1800 468 5736
- Daily 8–6
- MRT to Newton then SBS bus 171 or TIBS 182
- 5, 67, 75, 170, 171, 172, 173, 184
- None
- Free
- Visitor centre display and bookshop

17

SRI MARIAMMAN TEMPLE

HIGHLIGHTS

- *Gopuram*
- Thimithi festival
- Main doors
- Principal hall
- Ceiling frescoes
- Shrines

INFORMATION

- bII; E8
- 244 South Bridge Road
- 223 4064
- Daily 7AM–9PM
- Tanjong Pagar
- SBS bus 61, 103, 166, 197 from City Hall MRT
- None
- Free
- Chinatown (► 26)

A devotee burns incense in Sri Mariamman temple

This is Singapore's oldest Hindu temple, a technicolour shrine with brilliant statuary on the tower over the entrance. It is rather surprising to find it here – in the middle of Chinatown – but there has long been a Hindu temple on the site.

Origins The first temple was erected in 1827 by Nariana Pillai, Singapore's first Indian immigrant who became a successful trader and leader of the Hindu community. The original temple, made of wood and *atap* (nipa-palm leaves), was replaced by a brick structure in 1843. This building was later restored and extended. The temple is dedicated to the goddess Mariamman, who has powers to cure epidemics such as cholera and smallpox.

What to see This temple shows the three principal elements of Dravidian architecture: an interior shrine (*vimanam*) covered by a decorated dome, an assembly hall (*madapam*) used for prayers and an entrance tower (*gopuram*) covered with brightly painted Hindu deities. The splendid *gopuram* was not erected until 1903. The preferred venue of most Hindu weddings, the temple is also the focus for the annual Thimithi festival (► 22), when devotees

walk across a pit of glowing coals – supposedly painless – to honour the Hindu goddess Draupathi. The temple is still very much a place of worship and you must respect this and remember to remove your footwear before entering.

BUGIS STREET

Bugis Village, a very pale imitation of the original Bugis Street, offers a sanitised version of the street life found in other Asian cities. The clubs and market stalls abound, and pushy touts trap tourists into dining at expensive open-air restaurants.

Yesterday Bugis Street was the sin centre of old Singapore, the haunt of prostitutes and transvestites. Such activities were disapproved of by the Singaporean authorities, and the street was demolished in the 1980s to make way for the Bugis MRT station. Remembered with affection and sought out in vain by visitors, it was rebuilt in 1991, 137m from its original site. Six blocks of Chinese shophouses and some of the more celebrated original buildings were re-created and filled with pavement cafés and speciality shops.

Today The night market is open until late. Luxury goods, generally fake, tend to be sold near Victoria Street, and you can buy crafts and curios further down the road, fruit and vegetables near Albert Street. Around the edge of Bugis Village are several fast-food outlets, shops selling the latest fashions, a tea specialist and a traditional herbalist.

Bugis Junction Above Bugis MRT station is the 15-storey Bugis Junction complex, consisting of retail outlets, a cinema and office complex. The old Hylam street shophouse façades have been re-created in bright colours, and the whole street has been covered with a glass roof. Air-conditioning provides temperatures that remind one of temperate places, so visitors can shop or sit in one of the many cafés in comfort. The Hotel Inter-Continental adjoins the Bugis Junction complex.

HIGHLIGHTS

- Boutiques
- Bugis Junction
- Chinese herbalist
- Hylam Street
- Night market
- Open-air restaurants

INFORMATION

- ⊞ F6
- ✉ Bugis Street
- 🕐 Market open daily to midnight. Bars open daily to 2 or 3AM
- ✉ Albert Street
- 🕐 Mon–Fri 8:30pm–2am; Sat, Sun 8:30pm–3am
- 🍴 Open-air restaurants, fast-food outlets
- 🚇 Bugis
- 🚌 2, 5, 7, 12, 32, 61, 62, 63, 84, 130, 160, 197, 520, 851, 960
- ♿ Few (pedestrian precinct)
- 🛍 Moderate bars and food, antiques and crafts
- ↔ Little India (► 27), Kampung Glam (► 45)

19

SINGAPORE SCIENCE CENTRE

HIGHLIGHTS

- Atrium laser show
- Aviation Gallery
- Discovery Centre
- Hall of Information Technology
- Ecogarden
- Life Sciences Gallery
- Physical Sciences Gallery
- Omni Theatre

INFORMATION

- Off map to west
- 15 Science Centre Road
- 560 3316
- SSC Tue–Sun, public hols 10–6.
  Omni Theatre Tue–Sun, public hols 10–9
- Café in SSC, fast food in Omni Theatre
- Jurong East then 500m walk (turn left from station, along Block 135) or bus 335
- 66, 178, 198 direct; 51, 78, 197 to Jurong East Interchange then 335 or walk
- Good (space for 10 wheelchairs in Omni Theatre)
- Inexpensive
- Jurong BirdPark (➤ 33), Chinese and Japanese Gardens (➤ 56)

Hundreds of hands-on exhibits excite children, inspire teenagers and enlighten adults. The world of science and wonder awaits at the Singapore Science Centre that houses more than 600 exhibits.

Interactive exhibits The Singapore Science Centre opened its doors in 1977 and now attracts more than a million visitors each year. Exhibits in themed galleries offer fascinating insights into human achievements in the physical and life sciences. Many of the exhibits are interactive, and some are supported by talks and films.

Science to hand A laser light display welcomes you in the main lobby. The Aviation Gallery, introduces the principles of flight and examines how man first explored the skies. The Life Sciences Gallery focuses on the environment and people. You can walk through the internal organs of a human body in the Human Anatomy section. The Discovery Centre aims to stimulate the imagination of younger children with interactive displays, and the Ecogarden is informative for horticulturalists with its mini-orchard, hydroponic farm and medicinal garden. The Hall of Information Technology, opened in 1998, explains the role of communications in today's world.

Omni Theatre and Planetarium Next to the Science Centre is the Omni Theatre. This theatre has a five-storey-high, 23-m curved Omnimax screen, and state-of-the-art projection and audio equipment with surround sound. You can see films on subjects as diverse as climbing Mt Everest and the rule of China's first emperors. The features change every six months, so check to find out what's on during your visit.

MANDAI ORCHID GARDENS

Only rarely can nature be improved upon. But some of the orchid hybrids on display at these gardens are stunning, especially the **Vanda** *'Mandai Glow', with its beautiful blend of peach and pale orange.*

Cultivation Orchids have been grown on this site since 1951, when the land was leased by a couple of enthusiasts, John Laycock and Lee Kim Hong. It wasn't until 1956 that the gardens were turned into a commercial venture. Following Laycock's death, Amy Ede, his adopted daughter, managed the gardens. The area under cultivation has increased over the years to 4ha and today the orchid gardens are the largest on the island. Millions of sprays are exported all over the world each year, kept in good condition using a unique technology developed by the owners.

The orchids The gardens are packed with gorgeous blooms, some native, some introduced, as well as the many hybrids that have been the making of the Singapore orchid industry. Amazingly, despite the vast array of species on display, all orchids have the same shape – three sepals and three petals, but one of the petals, known as the 'lip', is a completely different shape from the others.

National flower The deep pink and white flowers of *Vanda* 'Miss Joaquim', Singapore's national flower, can be seen in abundance, as can many other varieties, including delicate slipper orchids and fantastic moth orchids. An hour's stroll in the gardens, which also contain a landscaped water garden, makes a gentle start to the day.

HIGHLIGHTS

- Early morning fragrance
- Black orchid
- Tiger orchid
- *Oncidium* 'Golden Shower'
- Torch ginger
- Jade vine

Mandai Orchid Gardens

INFORMATION

- ✛ Off map to northwest
- ✉ Mandai Lake Road
- ☎ 269 1036
- 🕐 Daily 8:30–5:30
- Ⓠ MRT to Ang Mo Kio then SBS bus 138
- 🚌 SBS bus 171 to Mandai Road then cross road for 138, or TIBS 927
- ♿ None
- 💵 Inexpensive
- ↔ Singapore Zoo (➤ 31), Night Safari (➤ 25)
- ❓ Boxed orchids can be sent abroad – details in shop

43

21

SINGAPORE ART MUSEUM

HIGHLIGHTS

- 19th-century building
- Large collection
- E-image gallery
- Library
- Museum
- Temporary exhibitions

INFORMATION

- E6
- 71 Bras Basah Road
- 375 2510
- Thu–Tue 9–5:30; Wed 9–9
- Dome café adjacent
- City Hall
- 14, 16, 36, 56, 82, 100, 107, 125, 167
- Few
- Inexpensive
- Fort Canning Park (➤ 34), Singapore History Museum (➤ 37)
- Free guided tours Tue–Fri 11AM, 2PM; Sat, Sun 11AM, 2PM, 3:30PM. Museum shop

With its focus on art of the 20th century, this is Singapore's flagship art museum dedicated to the collection and display of contemporary works from Singapore and Southeast Asia. It also presents visiting exhibitions.

National treasure The museum, opened in 1996, is housed in the restored 19th-century St Joseph's Insititution building, a former Catholic boys' school, and displays Singapore's national art collection. The permanent collection has grown from under 2,000 art works to over 4,000, and now houses the largest and most comprehensive collection of 20th-century Southeast Asian art in the region.

State of the art Almost 10,000sq metres of floor space include 14 galleries, a reference library, an auditorium, a multi-purpose hall, a museum shop, courtyards and an electronic E-image Gallery that runs interactive programmes featuring some of the museum's collection on a large visual monitor. Check out the nearby café that looks out over Queens Street.

On show Along with 'Imaging Selves', the Singapore Art Museum's first exhibition showcasing its permanent collection, the museum has also curated country focus exhibitions, 'From There to Now' and 'Soul Ties: The Land & Her People', focusing on Malaysia and Indonesia. An overview of Singaporean art is on permanent display and travelling exhibitions expose the region internationally. A community programme covers a diversity of art trends and practices, fringe activities and lectures. Check out Georgette Chen's striking *Self Portrait* (1934) and Chong Fah Cheong's tongue-in-cheek *Family and One* (1985).

KAMPUNG GLAM

The impressive golden domes and minarets of Sultan Mosque, glinting in the late afternoon sun, and the call of the muezzin, remind you that this area of Singapore is very much part of the Islamic world.

In the past Kampung Glam, where the Sultan of Singapore lived, was set aside in the early days for Malays, Arab, and Bugis traders. The 'Glam' may be named after the *gelam* tree from which medicinal oil was produced. Kampung Glam is now part of a designated conservation area.

Today Although there are 80 mosques on the island, Sultan Mosque is the focus of worship for Singapore's Muslim (mainly Malay) community. There has been a mosque on this site since 1824, when the East India Company made a grant for its construction. The present mosque dates from 1928, and reveals an interesting mix of Middle Eastern and Moorish influences. Its gilded dome is impressive; unusually, its base is made from bottles. Seen as you walk up Bussor-ah Street, with its shophouses at the rear, the mosque is truly stunning. Visitors are welcome outside prayer times, as long as they are well covered – no shorts. The *istana* (palace), built in the 1840s, is at the top of Sultan Gate and is well worth a look. The surrounding streets are good sources for *souk* items like basketware, perfume, batik and leather goods. The nearby Muslim coffee shops serve a wide range of Indian Muslim dishes such as *murtabak* (pancake with various fillings) and *mee goreng* (spicy fried noodles).

HIGHLIGHTS

- Bussorah Street
- Gilded dome of Sultan Mosque
- Prayer hall
- Istana Kampung Glam
- Murtabak
- Batik

INFORMATION

Sultan Mosque

- ✚ F6
- ✉ 3 Muscat Street
- ☎ 293 4405
- 🕐 Daily 11–7
- 🍴 Numerous coffee shops
- 🚇 Bugis
- 🚌 2, 32, 51, 61, 63, 84, 133, 145, 197
- ♿ None
- 🎫 Free
- ↔ Raffles Hotel (➤ 24), Bugis Street (➤ 41)

Rainbow hues for sale

EAST COAST PARK

HIGHLIGHTS

- Big Splash water rides
- Canoe hire
- East Coast Sailing Centre
- Parkland Golf Driving Range
- Tennis centre
- White-sand beaches

INFORMATION

➕ H6–N6

✉ East Coast Service Road

☎ ECSC 449 5118. Regent Bowl 443 1518. Tennis Centre 442 5966. Parkland Golf Range 440 6726. Big Splash 345 6762. Europa Disco 447 0869. Crocodilarium 447 3722. Ponggol Seafood 448 8511

🍴 East Coast Lagoon Food Rendezvous hawker centere (► 65), various kiosks, fast food at ECRC and Big Splash

🚇 Bedok then bus 401 or bus 31, 197; Eunos then 55, 155; Paya Lebar then 76, 135 and walk

🚌 16, 31, 55, 76, 135, 155, 196, 197, 853 daily to Marine Parade Road; 401 to East Coast Service Road (Sun)

♿ Some level paths

💲 Free; hire charges per hour for sports, etc.

↔ Changi Chapel (► 20), Joo Chiat Road (► 47)

Two decades of land reclamation have created this beachside playground. Swim or sail; walk, jog or cycle the 10km of tracks between coconut groves and bird sanctuaries; or laze on white sands with views of Indonesia's Riau Islands.

Plenty to do Picnicking families flock to the area on the weekends. There are many places to rent a bicycle, canoe, rollerblades or a deck chair, and it's a pleasant place to relax and catch a cooling breeze in the evening. The seafood centre at the Urban Development and Management Corporation (UDMC) clubhouse is popular with those who appreciate good seafood.

East Coast Sailing Centre Sailboards and laser dinghies can be hired here. If you encounter difficulties at sea, a rescue boat is on hand to bring you back to the East Coast Sailing Centre. The UDMC clubhouse has sports equipment for hire.

East Coast Recreation Centre Next to the park at the East Coast Recreation Centre are clay tennis courts (open until late evening), two bowling alleys and a snooker and billiards hall (open until the early hours). Golfers can prac-tice at the two-tier, 150m Parkland for just the cost of the balls. You can also hire bicycles, rollerblades and canoes. At the Big Splash, water rides delight adults and children alike, and in the same complex local bands entertain at the Europa Disco each evening.

Singapore Crocodilarium Approximately 1,000 crocodiles, crammed into concrete tanks, can be found at the Crocodilarium, where they are farmed. Crocodile-skin products are also show-cased in the shop here.

JOO CHIAT ROAD

Wonderful original architecture and intriguing old businesses by day, and an exciting mix of restaurants and music lounges in the evening, give a fascinating glimpse of former times and a sample of Singapore life today.

History The development of Katong was begun after World War I by Chew Joo Chiat. This once quiet seaside village is today an eclectic mix of colonial villas, Peranakan-style terraces and Malay bungalows. Some are preserved, many are being renovated, others remain untouched. The Joo Chiat Complex, at the northern end of Joo Chiat near the Malay Village Centre (▶ 75), is a busy local shopping complex selling fabrics and household goods at bargain prices. Next to the Village is the Geylang Serai market, a traditional Asian market, a good place to browse.

Eclectic mix Opposite Guan Hoe Soon Restaurant (which serves traditional Peranakan *nonya* dishes) is a typical 1920s corner terrace, with an ornate frieze of green dragons on the roof pediment. Terrace houses with covered walkways can be found along the road. The second storeys may be pillared verandas (No. 113), or have ornate casement windows (Nos. 370–6). Colourful tiles are a common feature (Nos. 137–9). Koon Seng Road, to the left, has two facing rows of bright terrace houses with courtyard gardens in front and extravagant mouldings, tiles and paintwork. Set in dense gardens are Malay-style elevated bungalows (Nos. 229, 382) fronted by verandas flanked by staircases. Villas to the southern end (Nos 507–9) indicate that this was the seafront before land reclamation. Turn left to the Katong Antique House (open by appointment), at No. 208, or right into East Coast Road.

HIGHLIGHTS

- Guan Hoe Soon Restaurant
- Joo Chiat Complex
- Katong Antique House
- Koon Seng Road
- Malay Village
- Malay-style bungalows
- Old seafront luxury villas
- Peranakan-style shophouses
- Residential terraces

INFORMATION

- ✚ L4–L5
- ✉ Joo Chiat Road
- ☎ Guan Hoe Soon 344 2761. Katong Antique House 345 8544
- 🍴 Guan Hoe Soon (*nonya* food, No. 214); Casa Bom Vento (No 47); Mum's Kitchen (No. 314); AJ Tandoori's (No. 328); Lemongrass (✉ 899 East Coast Road)
- Ⓢ Paya Lebar then walk
- 🚌 16, 33
- ♿ None
- 💲 Free
- ↔ East Coast Park (▶ 46)

47

25

BISHAN HDB ESTATE

INFORMATION

- ✚ Off map to north
- ✉ Bishan Central
- 🍴 3rd Mini Steamboat Delight
  9 Bishan Place, #04-01G
  and numerous other coffee
  shops, hawker centres and
  fast-food outlets
- 🚇 Bishan
- 🚌 13, 53, 54, 55, 56, 156
- ♿ Few
- ✋ Free

At a Bishan hawker centre

To get a feel of the Singapore you won't see in travel posters and catch a glimpse of the everday life of most Singaporeans, take a trip to the public housing estates, where most locals live, eat, socialise and shop. Bishan will give you the overall picture.

Public Housing More than 80 per cent of Singapore's population lives in state-subsidised Housing and Development Board apartments known as HDBs. Hundreds of these government-built blocks exist in any given area, each a small town in its own right. Bishan, developed in the early 1990s, adds to the steadily growing list of these distinctive housing estates.

See how most locals live As with most HDB areas, Bishan has its own MRT station, around which a shopping and entertainment complex, Junction 8, has been built. Wander around Junction 8's central area close to the MRT station, up Bishan Road, and from there turn right in front of the MRT, then left into Street 22. You'll come upon one of the many smaller satellite community areas, complete with its own shops and hawker centre at the base of the housing blocks. On the outskirts of Bishan, at Bright Hill Drive, is Phor Kark See, a huge Buddhist temple overlooking Bishan Park.

When to visit The best times to visit are in early morning, when housewives are out shopping, and in early evening, when families get together to shop and have their evening meal at the hawker centre. Try a steamboat meal – fish, meat and vegetables that diners cook in pots of boiling broth at their table – either at a hawker centre or at 3rd Mini Steamboat Delight near Bishan bus interchange behind the main shopping complex.

SINGAPORE's
best

MODERN ARCHITECTURE

Going up!

Don't miss the ride in the high-speed lift of the Westin Stamford Hotel – the only way to get to the top of its 73 storeys. A matter of seconds after leaving the ground floor you are deposited 226m in the air.

The Ritz-Carlton Millennia Hotel

See Top 25 Sights for
ORCHARD ROAD (➤ 30)

THE GATEWAY (1990)

The twin towers of this office development – 37 storeys of darkly tinted glass – dominate this area between Ophir Road and Rochor Canal Road. The structure, with a distinctive gap in the middle, was loosely inspired by traditional Balinese split gates.

➕ F6 ✉ 152 Beach Road 🚇 City Hall 🎟 Free

RITZ-CARLTON MILLENNIA HOTEL (1995)

Singapore's most stylish 22-storey-high luxury hotel is built on reclaimed land in Marina Bay. The glass-domed roof of the lobby is a key feature, and the grandeur understated.

➕ F7 ✉ 7 Raffles Avenue ☎ 337 8888 🍴 Six restaurants 🚇 Raffles City 🎟 Free

SINGAPORE MARRIOTT (1982)

This 33-storey hotel is rare among modern buildings, with its octagonal structure and fanciful pagoda-style roof. Its unusual appearance makes it a striking local landmark.

➕ C5 ✉ 320 Orchard Road ☎ 735 5800 🍴 Four restaurants 🚇 Orchard 🎟 Free

SUNTEC CITY (1995)

Singapore International Convention and Exhibition Centre, in Suntec City along Temasek Boulevard, built according to *feng shui* principles, alongside office towers, and with the world's largest fountain.

➕ F7 ✉ 3 Temasek Boulevard ☎ 337 3803 🕐 Daily 10–10 🍴 Numerous restaurants 🚇 City Hall 🎫 Free

UOB PLAZA (1996)

The 66-storey UOB Plaza building at the bottom of Boat Quay is impressively out of scale with the small shophouses along the river. At 280m, it is as high as Singapore building regulations allow.

➕ dII; E8 ✉ 80 Raffles Place, UOB Plaza 1 ☎ 533 9898 🍴 Top of the Plaza Cantonese restaurant 🚇 Raffles Place 🎫 Free

WESTIN STAMFORD HOTEL (1985)

At 226m (with 73 storeys), this is one of the world's tallest hotels. The Compass Rose Bar and Restaurant, at the top, allows fantastic views over much of the island.

➕ F7 ✉ 2 Stamford Road, Raffles City ☎ 338 8585 🍴 Seven restaurants 🚇 City Hall 🎫 Free

WHEELOCK PLACE (1993)

This chic glass and stone structure contains one of the island's many shopping complexes. The glass pyramid fronting Orchard Road is a unique addition along this busy thoroughfare.

➕ C5 ✉ 501 Orchard Road 🕐 Daily 10–10 🍴 Four cafés 🚇 Orchard 🎫 Free

Going outwards

The northern loop of Singapore's state-of-the-art metro system, the mass rapid transit (MRT), was completed in 1987. An ambitious five-year project, to build the North-East Line, which will link the World Trade Centre with Punggol, is now well under way and due to be completed in 2002.

The 66-storey UOB Plaza

COLONIAL STYLE

Watering holes

Try the Somerset Bar in the Westin Stamford Hotel for evening drinks and live jazz. Alternatively, there is the fabled Long Bar at Raffles, where, amazingly in litter-free Singapore, the tradition is to throw your empty peanut shells on the floor.

See Top 25 Sights for
RAFFLES HOTEL (► 24)
THE PADANG (► 35)

CHIJMES

Chijmes started life as a convent, girls' school and orphanage in 1854. The convent closed in 1983 and the buildings were developed in the mid-1990s to house shops, bars and restaurants. The chapel is now called Chijmes Hall and is well worth a visit.

➕ E6 ✉ 30 Victoria Street 🔲 City Hall 🏮 Free

COLONIAL RESIDENCES

A walk along Cluny, Lermit and Nassim roads, between the west end of Orchard Road and the Botanic Gardens, will give glimpses of 19th-century colonial residences. These mansions come equipped for making living in the tropical heat as tolerable as possible: enormous blinds, shaded balconies and verandas, and rich, landscaped gardens.

➕ A5–B5 ✉ Cluny, Lermit and Nassim roads 🔲 Orchard 🏮 Free

GOODWOOD PARK HOTEL

This building, erected in 1900, started life as the Teutonia Club for Singapore's German population. Although there have been many alterations, the façade has remained unchanged with its pretty turrets. It was converted into a hotel after World War II.

➕ C5 ✉ 22 Scotts Road ☎ 737 7411 🍴 Eight restaurants 🔲 Orchard 🏮 Free

POLO CLUB

Although the Polo Club is a little way out of town, its veranda makes a pleasant place for enjoying a sundowner and dinner as the light fades over the polo field (rapidly in the tropics). Worth a visit especially as non-members are allowed entry to the bar and the restaurant.

➕ D2 ✉ 80 Mount Pleasant Road ☎ 256 4530 🕐 Daily 8–11 🍴 Restaurant, bar 🚌 54, 130, 132, 156, 166 🏮 Free

Action at the Singapore Polo Club

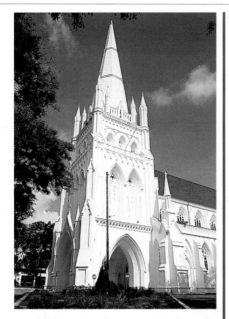

Singapore Sling

This cocktail, closely associated with Singapore, has been served since 1910 – and given the thousands Raffles alone serves every week, that's a lot of slings. It's a sweet mixture of gin, cherry brandy, maraschino cordial, lemon juice, sugar and angostura bitters. It's served in all the big hotels, but the place to say you've drunk it is in the Long Bar of Raffles Hotel.

The starkly white, Gothic-style St Andrew's Cathedral

RAFFLES HOTEL – BILLIARDS

Billiards was a favourite sport in colonial times. The famed Bar and Billiards Room at Raffles Hotel houses a 100-year-old table (under which a tiger is said to have once been seen) and also serves the famous Singapore Sling – an excellent way to unwind after a day of sightseeing.

✛ F6 ✉ 1 Beach Road ☎ 337 1886 🍴 Several restaurants (► 24) ⏱ Tiffin served daily noon–2 and 7–10 🚇 City Hall

RAFFLES HOTEL – TIFFIN

Tiffin is the light meal originally taken at midday by colonial officials in India; a mixture of English and Asian fare was usually served. Today the delicious tiffin buffet available at lunch and dinner in the Tiffin Room of the Raffles Hotel recalls the colonial custom.

✛ F6 ✉ 1 Beach Road ☎ 337 1886 🍴 Several restaurants (► 24) ⏱ Tiffin served daily noon–2 and 7–10 🚇 City Hall

ST ANDREW'S CATHEDRAL

Completed in 1861, St Andrew's was the focus of Anglican religious life during colonial times and is still a popular place of worship. It was built by convict Indian labour and the whiter-than-white exterior is said to have been achieved by the use of Madras *chunan* – a mixture of shell lime, egg white and sugar – commonly used in India.

✛ E7 ✉ St Andrew's Road ☎ 337 6104 ⏱ Daily 8–6 🚇 City Hall ⛪ Free

Evening tradition

An early evening drive round the Padang and games of cricket on the pitch were traditions that were faithfully respected by the colony's early administrators – however hot the weather.

53

MUSEUMS & PLACES OF WORSHIP

Dragons

Dragons are a common symbol in Chinese temples, and represent the opposing forces of *yin* and *yang*. In Thian Hock Keng Temple (➤ 26), they can be seen on the roof ridges and the huge granite pillars near the entrance.

Gold dragon in Thian Hock Keng Temple

See Top 25 Sights for
ASIAN CIVILISATIONS MUSEUM (➤ 28)
SINGAPORE ART MUSEUM (➤ 44)
SINGAPORE HISTORY MUSEUM (➤ 37)
SULTAN MOSQUE, KAMPUNG GLAM (➤ 46)

MUSEUMS

FUK TAK CHI MUSEUM

This was the first Chinese temple in Singapore. The temple originally stood right on the waterfront. Newly arrived Chinese immigrants would hop off their boat after a long hard voyage and go straight into the temple to thank the gods for a safe passage, and to ask for prosperity in business. Thanks to land reclamation, it now stands in the middle of Far East Square on the edge of the financial district.

➕ dJ; E8 ✉ Telok Ayer Street ☎ 227 7531 (Far East Square) 🚇 Raffles Place 🎫 Free

ISTANA BESAR

In neighbouring Johor Bahru, the Sultan's Palace is now a fascinating museum that traces the history of the local royal family. You can visit the throne room, the family bedrooms and banquet halls and view many displays.

➕ Off map to north ✉ Jalan Ayer Molek ☎ 223 0555 🕐 Sat–Thu 10-5 🚌 170 🎫 Moderate

RAFFLES MUSEUM

This charming small museum was set up when hotel re-opened after renovation in 1991. Artefacts and memorabilia associated with the hotel were gathered together from its own collection and by advertising. The result is a delightful display of early plans and photographs, personal letters and postcards (some from well-known guests), luggage labels, travel posters and the like.

➕ F6 ✉ Raffles Hotel Arcade ☎ 337 1886 🕐 Daily 10–7 🍴 Many nearby in Raffles Hotel and Raffles City 🚇 City Hall 🎫 Free

PLACES OF WORSHIP

ARMENIAN CHURCH

The Church of St Gregory the Illuminator was built in 1835 for the small Armenian community that even at this early date had already been attracted to the growing port of Singapore. It has the distinction of being the oldest surviving Christian church in Singapore, and is still used as a place of worship. There are occasional services, and times are posted on the notice board at the entrance.

🔲 E7 ✉ 60 Hill Street ☎ 334 0141 🕐 Daily 8–8 🚇 City Hall 🎫 Free

CHETTIAR TEMPLE

The temple of Sri Thandayuthanapani, rebuilt in 1984, is also called Chettiar Temple after the Indian *chettiars* (moneylenders) who financed its construction in the 1850s. The *gopuram* is a riot of images and colours. Each glass panel of the unusual 48-panel ceiling frieze, brought from India, features a deity from the Hindu pantheon.

🔲 D6 ✉ 15 Tank Road ☎ 737 9393 🕐 Daily 8–noon, 5:30–8:30 🚇 Dhoby Ghaut 🎫 Free

Detail of the gopuram *of Chettiar Temple*

NAGORE DURGHA SHRINE

This undeniably picturesque small mosque close to Thian Hock Keng Temple was built around 1820 for the Indian Muslim community by Chulias, southern Indian Muslims from the Coromandel Coast. Painted in white and green, it has tiny minarets and a façade of small archways and delicate plaster grilles.

🔲 cII; E8 ✉ 140 Telok Ayer Street ☎ 324 0021 🕐 Daily 10–10 🚇 Raffles Place 🎫 Free

SRI SRINIVASA PERUMAL TEMPLE

Like many of the Hindu temples in Singapore, this temple has a *gopuram*, a main worshipping hall, and a shrine for the gods. The *gopuram* was built in 1979, funded by a leading Singapore merchant, P Govindasamy Pillai, whose name also appears over one or two of the shops in Little India.

🔲 F4 ✉ Serangoon Road ☎ 298 5771 🕐 Daily 6–noon, 6–9 🚇 Bugis 🎫 Free

Singapore's national flower

The orchid *Vanda* 'Miss Joaquim' – a natural hybrid – is named after Agnes Joaquim, a Dutch expatriate, who discovered it one morning in 1893 growing in her garden. She is buried in the small graveyard of the Armenian Church (➤ 54).

55

GARDENS & GREEN SPACES

What's in a name?

The Chinese Garden is full of romantically named sites: Cloud-Piercing Pagoda, Courtyard of Early Spring, Moon Inviting Boat and Tiger's Roar Waterfall. With romance in the air, the gardens are popular with young couples as a backdrop for wedding photographs.

See Top 25 Sights for
BOTANIC GARDENS (► 29)
BUKIT TIMAH NATURE RESERVE (► 39)
FORT CANNING PARK (► 34)
MANDAI ORCHID GARDENS (► 43)

CHINATOWN AND TANJONG PAGAR

If you feel like a little tranquility after the hustle and bustle of Chinatown, find the path (backing Bukit Pasoh and Craig roads) that runs between New Bridge Road, opposite Pearl Centre, and Tanjong Pagar. Shady trees and handy benches line the route, which takes you past renovated shophouses and a Buddhist temple and brings you out at Tanjong Pagar food centre.

🔁 blll; D8 ✉ Bukit Pasoh and Craig roads

CHINESE AND JAPANESE GARDENS

Chinese and Japanese classical gardens have been created on two islands in Jurong Lake. The Chinese Garden covers 13ha and is dotted with pagodas, pavilions and arched bridges. The main building is based on Beijing's Summer Palace. During the mid-autumn festival the gardens are hung with lanterns. The Japanese Gardens are altogether more serene, and take their inspiration from gardens of the 15th to 17th centuries.

🔁 Off map to west ✉ 1 Chinese Garden Road ☎ 264 3455
🕐 Daily 9–6:30 🍴 Refreshment kiosks 🚇 Chinese Garden
🎫 Inexpensive

A pagoda in the Chinese Garden

MACRITCHIE RESERVOIR PARK

You can jog or walk on the shaded paths around the reservoir's edge; there are exercise stations at intervals. From the bridge you can watch turtles and carp, and, if it's switched on, you'll see the fountain, which features 30 water-jet patterns. Concerts take place in the pavilion. Look for monkeys, but don't feed them.

🔁 C1 ✉ Lornie Road 🕐 24 hours
🍴 Food kiosk 🚇 MRT to Newton
then bus 104, 132 or 167 🎫 Free

MOUNT FABER PARK

Rewarding views of Keppel Harbour, Sentosa Island and, on clear days, some of the Indonesian Riau Islands can be seen

from the top of Mount Faber, a signal station in the 19th century. The park's 73ha have been planted with a variety of trees and shrubs; the bougainvillea, which flower year-round in Southeast Asia, particularly stand out. A cable car connects the top of Mount Faber to the World Trade Centre (WTC) and Sentosa Island.

➕ B9 ✉ Mount Faber Road 🕐 24 hours 🍽 Café 🚇 MRT to City Hall then bus 61, 124, 143 or 166 🎫 Free

St John's Island

PASIR RIS PARK

This 71-ha area contains some of Singapore's last remaining stretches of mangrove swamp, and is now a bird and nature reserve. Raised boardwalks meander through this habitat. Look for fiddler crabs, mudskippers and small-clawed otters. Birds you might spot include herons, yellow-vented bulbuls, brown-throated sunbirds and collared kingfishers. The best way to explore is by bicycle and there are a couple of places that rent out moutain bikes.

➕ Off map to northeast ✉ Off Jalan Loyang Kecil 🕐 24 hours 🚇 MRT to Pasir Ris then bus 403 🎫 Free

PULAU UBIN ISLAND (► 20)

ST JOHN'S ISLAND

This relatively unspoiled island is good for walking and picnicking. People do swim and relax on the beaches, but water conditions – as with most in Singapore – are not ideal as the island is in the middle of one of the world's busiest shipping routes. At weekends, volleyball is popular.

➕ Off map to south ☎ 270 3918 for ferry details 🍽 Café 🚢 Ferry from World Trade Centre (Mon–Sat 10AM, 1:30PM; six sailings on Sun from 9:45AM) 🎫 Ferry tickets moderate

SUNGEI BULOH NATURE RESERVE (► 20)

Mangroves – unique adaptations

Mangrove plants have adapted to salty, swampy conditions. Some species have 'breathing roots', called pneumatophores, others a tangle of aerial roots. These allow the plant to take in more oxygen, which helps it eliminate the salt absorbed from the water. You can see mangroves at Sungei Buloh and Pasir Ris reserves.

57

Parascending is just one of the many sports possible in Singapore

OUTDOOR ACTIVITIES

ARCHERY

ARCHERY TRAINING CENTRE
The only centre for archery aficionados and anyone wishing to take up the sport. It has a range that allows shooting up to 70m.

✚ D2 ✉ Singapore Polo Club, 80 Mount Pleasant Road ☎ 760 1300 🕐 Daily 9–6 🚌 160, 166, 167, 605, 851 💰 Expensive. Courses charged for six lessons

BICYCLE HIRE

SDK RECREATION
Bike hire is available near the East Coast Recreation Centre, and one of many kiosks along the 3-km East Coast Parkway cycle track. Lights and some safety equipment also available.

✚ Off map to east ✉ 1000 East Coast Parkway, #01-00 ☎ 445 2969/241 5214 🕐 Mon–Fri 10–8; Sat 9–8; pub hols 8–8 🍴 Cafés and restaurants nearby 🚇 Bedok then bus 401; Eunos then bus 55 or 155 💰 Moderate

SENTOSA CYCLING SERVICES
Renting a bike on Sentosa Island, with its many bicycle paths, is a relaxing way of getting some exercise, though the routes are popular at weekends.

✚ Off map to south ✉ Sentosa Bicycle Station ☎ 272 8676 🕐 9:30–6:30 🍴 Various food outlets 🚇 (▶ 32) 💰 Expensive

FLYING

REPUBLIC OF SINGAPORE FLYING CLUB
Plane rental and lessons are available. If it's panoramic aerial views you're after, ask about sightseeing flights.

✚ Off map to north ✉ Seletar Air Base, Jalan Kayu, Building 140B, East Camp ☎ 481 0502 🕐 Daily 9–5:30 🚇 Yio Chu Kang then bus 59, 214E 💰 Expensive

GOLF

LAGUNA NATIONAL GOLF & COUNTRY CLUB
This club has two full golf courses: a 6,504m, par 73; and a 6,210m, par 72. There is also a 550m-, par 54 putting course with 18 holes. Amenities include a swimming pool, children's playground and playroom, tennis, billiards and a gymnasium. Saturday is members only, but you can call and see if there is a free slot.

✚ Off map to east ✉ 11 Laguna Golf Green ☎ 542 6888 🕐 Daily 7–7 🍴 Restaurant, café 🚇 Tanah Merah 💰 Expensive

A day out on the fairway

The Laguna Club has probably the most extensive golf facilities in Singapore, and possibly in Asia. It has two championship 18-hole courses designed by Andy Dye, a driving range and a chipping green, all beautifully landscaped on reclaimed land. The resort's facilities, centred around the clubhouse, make for a pleasant day out even for non-golfing friends and family members.

SELETAR COUNTRY CLUB

This is one of the handful of country clubs open to non-Singapore residents on weekends. It features a nine-hole, 2,885m, par 35 course beside Seletar Reservoir in the north of the island.

➕ Off map to north ✉ 101 Seletar Club Road ☎ 481 4812 🕐 Daily 9–10 🍴 Restaurant 🚍 59, 103 or 163, then 214 💰 Expensive

ICE-SKATING

ICE WORLD KALLANG

Although it can be crowded on weekends, this rink has reasonable rates and classes for novices.

➕ H6 ✉ 5 Stadium Walk, #03-06 ☎ 348 7928 🕐 Mon–Wed, Fri and Sat 10–10; Thu and Sun 10–9 🚍 11, 16 💰 Moderate

SCUBA DIVING

MARSDEN BROS DIVE SCHOOL

Marsden Bros have the only custom-made dive boat in Singapore and offer excellent PADI (Professional Association of Diving Instructors) dive courses. They run to Singapore's southern reefs around Pulau Hantu and Pulau Salu.

➕ Off map to west ✉ 113 Holland Road (by Farrer Road flyover) ☎ 475 0050 🚍 5, 7, 61, 75, 77, 105, 106, 123, 156, 165, 174, 200 💰 Expensive

SENTOSA WATERSPORTS CENTRE

Dive trips, day-trips, lessons, and diving equipment sales and rentals. Equipment for a variety of other watersports is also available to hire.

➕ B10 ✉ 1 Maritime Square, #01-06, World Trade Centre ☎ 274 5612 🕐 Daily 9–7 🍴 Various outlets in World Trade Centre 🚃 (▶ 32) 💰 Expensive

WINDSURFING & SAILING

EUROPA SAILING CLUB

Basic equipment can be rented here and lessons are also available. The club has a bar, shop and café. Beach barbecues on Sunday and Wednesday evenings.

➕ Off map to east ✉ East Coast Sailing Lagoon, 1212 East Coast Parkway ☎ 449 5118 🕐 10–5 (café closed Mon) 🍴 Café, restaurant, barbecues 🚍 Bedok then bus 31 or 197 💰 Moderate

Taking to the waters

With the Riau Islands and the ships in the strait seaward, and the palm-fringed East Coast Park backed by luxury condominiums landward, sailing from the East Coast offers spectacular views. Winds are often best in mid-afternoon, but currents can be strong. The best days end when you come ashore to a barbecue on the beach and the music of a live band.

Watersports are popular in the warm seas around Singapore

FOR CHILDREN

See Top 25 Sights for
JURONG BIRD PARK (➤ 33)
NIGHT SAFARI (➤ 25)
SINGAPORE SCIENCE CENTRE (➤ 42)
SINGAPORE ZOO (➤ 31)

Ring of fire

Although it lies very close to some of the world's most active volcanoes (in Indonesia), Singapore itself has no volcanic activity. Not, that is, until 1994, when an active volcano miraculously appeared on an island just south of Singapore – part of VolcanoLand, an attraction on Sentosa (➤ 32). Not to worry, it poses no hazard despite 'erupting' every 30 minutes.

BORDERS BOOKSHOP

Borders has a children's section with an atmosphere that encourages kids to pick up books and read on the spot. Author story-telling sessions for children are regular events – look on the notice board at the main entrance for details. There is also a restaurant and a café, and CDs as well as books.

➕ C5 ✉ 501 Orchard Road ☎ 235 7146 🕐 Sun–Thu 9–11; Fri, Sat 9–midnight 🍴 Café and restaurant 🚇 Orchard

LAU PA SAT (TELOK AYER MARKET)

This octagonal cast-iron structure, originally a fish market, was built more than 100 years ago from pieces shipped out from Scotland. It has been renovated and now houses stalls and kiosks devoted to selling a variety of Asian fare, from Mongolian grilled meats to Hainanese beef noodles. Apart from the food, you'll find stalls selling regional handicrafts such as Balinese carvings and Chinese silks.

➕ dIII; E8 ✉ 18 Raffles Quay 🕐 24 hrs 🍴 Foodstalls 🚇 Raffles Place

MING VILLAGE

Here, artist craftsmen use age-old techniques to recreate the porcelain of the Ming and Qing dynasties. You can view traditional Chinese porcelain making processes including mould-making, hand-throwing, glazing, hand-painting and firing, under a single roof. Guided tours are daily from 9AM to 5:30PM, and a good selection of products is on sale.

➕ Off map to west ✉ 32 Pandan Road, Jurong ☎ 265 7711 🕐 Daily 19–5.30 🍴 Restaurants 🚇 MRT to Clementi then bus 78 🎫 Free

Tea-time at Singapore Zoo

UNDERWATER WORLD (SENTOSA)

In Asia's largest aquarium, a moving walkway takes you through a dome-shaped glass tunnel, while hundreds of species of the region's sea creatures swim above and around you. This is the closest many people ever get to a living coral reef. Look for the starfish, sharks, poisonous lionfish and beautiful weedy sea dragons.

➕ Off map to south ✉ 80 Siloso Road ☎ 275 0030 🕐 Daily 9–9 🍴 Restaurant 🚇 (➤ 32). Bus or monorail from main ferry terminal on Sentosa 🎫 Moderate

SINGAPORE
where to...

CHINESE

Prices

For dinner per person for three courses, without drinks, expect to pay appoximately:

£	up to S$20
££	S$20–S$40
£££	more than S$40

Hokkien variation on a spring roll

Popiah – freshly prepared rice-flour pancakes filled with a mouthwatering mixture of onion, turnip, bean sprouts, minced pork and prawns, all held together with a sweet soy sauce and flavoured with coriander, garlic and chili – makes a delicious snack. You can order *popiah* in some restaurants, and many hawker centres have a *popiah* stall.

Steamboat

Not a form of transport, rather a delicious method of tableside cooking where a selection of fish, meat and vegetables is placed in a container of boiling broth, you can cook it to your liking and retrieve it with chopsticks when it's achieved perfect doneness.

BENG THIN HOON KEE (££)

Hokkien food is popular in Singapore, for the ancestors of many Singaporeans lived in southern China, where the cuisine originated. Try duck in lotus leaves.

✚ cll; E7 ☒ #05-02 OCBC Building, 65 Chulia Street ☎ 533 7708 🕐 Daily 11–12:45, 6–9:45 🚇 Raffles Place

CHARMING GARDEN (££)

Hunan and Szechuan specialities include fried yam rolls, steamed minced pigeon and dragon bearded prawns.

✚ C4 ☒ Copthorne Orchid Singapore, 214 Dunearn Road ☎ 251 8149 🕐 Daily 11:30–2:30, 6:30–10:30 🚇 Newton

FATTY'S EATING HOUSE (££)

A local institution with an extensive Cantonese menu. Everything is well cooked and speedily delivered.

✚ E5 ☒ #01-33 Albert Complex, Albert Street ☎ 338 1087 🕐 Daily 12–2:30, 5:30–10 🚇 Bugis

IMPERIAL HERBAL RESTAURANT (£££)

Ants and scorpions, anyone? You'll find them on the menu here.

✚ F6 ☒ Metropole Hotel, 41 Seah Street ☎ 337 0491 🕐 Daily 11:30–2:30, 6:30–10:30 🚇 City Hall

MIN JIANG SICHUAN RESTAURANT (££)

Classic spicy Szechuan food is served here, such as tea-smoked duck and drunken chicken.

✚ C5 ☒ Goodwood Park Hotel, 22 Scotts Road ☎ 737 7411 🕐 Daily 12–2:30, 6:30–10:30 🚇 Orchard

MOSQUE STREET STEAMBOAT HOUSE & RESTAURANT (££)

Steamboat is good value and great fun.

✚ blll; E8 ☒ 44 Mosque Street ☎ 222 9560 🕐 Daily 6–4AM 🚇 Tanjong Pagar

THE RED BOOK (££)

Revolutionary modern Asian food sets the theme at this place. Chairman Mao memorabilia adorns the walls and staff wear Red Guard uniforms.

✚ C5 ☒ #01/09-10 442 Orchard Road ☎ 733 7667 🕐 Daily 11:30–2:30, 6:30–10:30 🚇 Orchard

WAK LOK CANTONESE RESTAURANT (££)

Fine Cantonese dinners and tasty dim sum lunches. Hong Kong Chinese come here to eat.

✚ E6 ☒ Carlton Hotel, 76 Bras Basah Road ☎ 330 3588 🕐 Mon–Sat 11:30–2:30, 6:30–10:30; Sun 11–2:30, 6:30–10:30 🚇 City Hall

WEE NAM KEE (£)

Here you can get an excellent version of one of the most popular local dishes, Hainanese chicken rice – chicken meat with rice and broth.

✚ D3 ☒ 275 Thomson Road ☎ 256 4051 🕐 Daily 10AM–2AM 🚇 Novena

INDIAN

ANNALAKSHMI (££)

This Indian vegetarian restaurant is part of an Indian arts foundation. The buffet is good value and includes interesting dips made from mustard and coconut. Try the delicious *lassi*, a yoghurt drink.

✚ E7 ✉ #02-10 Excelsior Hotel Shopping Centre, 5 Coleman Street ☎ 339 9993 ⏰ Mon–Sat 11:30–3, 6–10 🚇 City Hall

BANANA LEAF APOLLO (££)

A southern Indian 'banana-leaf' restaurant the leaf takes the place of a plate – with a good range of dishes to accompany the vegetable curries.

✚ E5 ✉ 54 Race Course Road ☎ 293 8682 ⏰ Daily 10:30–10 🚇 Bugis

KINARA (££)

Food, from northern India, is served in what looks like the inside of a Rajasthani fort. Eating here is memorable. The food is good, though helpings can be small.

✚ dI; E7 ✉ 57 Boat Quay ☎ 533 0412 ⏰ Mon–Fri 11:30–2:30, 6:30–10:30; Sat–Sun 6:30–10:45 🚇 Raffles Place

KOMALA VILAS (£)

Southern Indian fare is served here on banana leaves. It's good and inexpensive, and you can have unlimited helpings of the vegetarian food. Basic meals include vegetable curries and rice with side dishes of dhal and *dosai* (thin pancakes).

For a different drink, try the sweet, spicy *masala* tea.

✚ E5 ✉ 76 Serangoon Road ☎ 293 6980 ⏰ Daily 7AM–10:30PM 🚇 Bugis

MUTHU'S CURRY HOUSE (££)

Vegetable curries are dished out fast and furiously to accompany meat, crab, squid or fish. Try the famous fish-head curry.

✚ E5 ✉ 78 Race Course Road ☎ 293 2389 ⏰ Daily 10–10 🚇 Bugis

NIRVANA (££)

This is the sister restaurant of the famed Moti Mahal on Murray Street, and offers a similar menu of north Indian tandoori dishes.

✚ F4 ✉ 2 Owen Road ☎ 297 0400 ⏰ Daily 11:30–2:30, 6:30–10:30 (closed Tuesday evenings) 🚇 Lavender

OUR VILLAGE (££)

North and northwest Indian food is prepared 'village style' here. Try the *handi gosht*, a lamb curry, and the tasty desserts.

✚ dI; E7 ✉ 5th Floor, 46 Boat Quay ☎ 538 3092 ⏰ Daily 11:30–1:30, 6–10:30 🚇 Bugis

RANG MAHAL (£££)

A good range of north Indian dishes and an extensive buffet at both lunch and dinner. Indian dance performances are a feature here.

✚ D6 ✉ Imperial Hotel, 1 Jalan Rumbia ☎ 737 1666 ⏰ Daily 12–2:30, 7–11 🚇 Dhoby Ghaut

Hand or cutlery?

Many Hindus and Muslims eat their food with the right hand only; it is considered unclean to eat with the left hand, although it's okay to use utensils – usually a fork and spoon. Eating with your hand, you tear pieces of chapati (using only one hand) and then soak or scoop up elements of the meal. For rice there's another technique: you add the curries and work up the into balls which you then pick up and pop – almost flick – into your mouth.

OTHER ASIAN FARE

'Satay! Satay!'

No trip to Singapore would be complete without the famous *satay*, a Malay dish. Sticks of chicken, lamb or beef, and sometimes other foods such as tofu, are barbecued and served with a thick, sweet peanut sauce. Small rice cakes and cucumber usually accompany the satay. It is served in some restaurants, and at many hawker centres there is a '*satay man*'. If you develop a taste for it, look in supermarkets for the ready-made *satay* sauce and try it at home with a barbecue.

ALKAFF MANSION (£££)

A 1920s colonial house atop a hill has been turned into a charming restaurant serving international cuisine, Peranakan cuisine and *rijstaffel* – Indonesian-Dutch buffet. Expensive but worth it. ᕀ A8 ✉ 10 Telok Blangah Green ☎ 278 6979 🕐 Daily 12–2:30, 3–5:30, 7–10:30 🚇 124, 143, 166

HAE BOK'S KOREAN RESTAURANT (££)

Reliably good Korean dishes such as fried octopus with Korean spicy sauce and fried, egg-coated vegetables. ᕀ C7 ✉ 405 Havelock Road #02-20 ☎ 735 4440 🕐 Daily 11:30–3, 5:30–10:30 🚇 Tiong Bahru

HOUSE OF SUNDANESE FOOD (££)

Spicy food from west Java – the fish dishes are particularly good. The original restaurant is at 218 East Coast Road (☎ 345 5020) and a newer outlet is in Suntec City mall basement (☎ 334 1012 ▶ 51). ᕀ dl; E7 ✉ 55 Boat Quay ☎ 534 3775 🕐 Mon–Fri 11–2; Sat 12–2:30, 6–10 🚇 Raffles Place

INAGIKU (£££)

Four sections serve excellent tempura, *teppanyaki* and sushi. Top prices but also a less expensive à la carte menu. ᕀ F6 ✉ 3rd floor, Westin Plaza Hotel, 2 Stamford Road ☎ 338 8585 🕐 Mon–Sat

12–2:30, 6:30–10:30 🚇 City Hall

NONYA AND BABA (££)

Dishes such as *otak-otak* (fish cake in banana leaves) and *itek tim* (duck soup) are typical examples of *nonya* food (a fusion of Chinese and Malay cuisines). The rice- and coconut-based desserts are worth trying. ᕀ D6 ✉ 262 River Valley Road ☎ 734 1382 🕐 Daily 11–3, 6–10 🚇 Dhoby Ghaut 🚇 32, 54, 195

SUNTORY (££)

This established Japanese restaurant serves excellent sushi, tempura and *shabu-shabu*. Expensive but good. ᕀ C5 ✉ #06-01 Delfi Orchard, 402 Orchard Road ☎ 732 5111 🕐 Daily 12–1:45, 6:30–9:45 🚇 Orchard

TAMBUAH MAS (££)

Very good Indonesian food – don't miss the *ikan bilis* (whitebait and peanuts) and *soto ayam* (thick chicken soup) – almost Java's national dish. A branch is at the Shaw Centre. ᕀ B5 ✉ #04-10 Tanglin Shopping Centre, 19 Tanglin Road ☎ 733 2220 🕐 Daily 10–11 🚇 Orchard

THANYING (££)

This Thai restaurant is always packed. Try the green curries and stuffed chicken wings. ᕀ blv; D9 ✉ Amara Hotel, 165 Tanjong Pagar Road ☎ 222 4688 🕐 Mon–Sat 11:30–3, 6:30–11 🚇 Tanjong Pagar

HAWKER CENTRES

CHINA SQUARE (£)

This sprawling three-storey food complex has Western food outlets and traditional hawker fare under one roof.

cll; E8 ✉ Telok Ayer Street ⏰ Daily 7AM–10PM 🚇 Raffles Place

CHINATOWN COMPLEX FOOD CENTRE (£)

In this large, always buzzing food centre in the middle of Chinatown, most types of local Chinese food are available as is a wide range of desserts – try the ice *kacang*.

bll; ✉ Chinatown Complex, Smith Street ⏰ Early till late daily 🚇 Outram Park

EAST COAST LAGOON FOOD CENTRE (£)

The good food and sea breezes make this popular. The *satay* is very good, as are the *laksa* and any number of tantalising seafood dishes including chili or black pepper crab, and cuttlefish.

Off map to east ✉ East Coast Parkway ⏰ Late morning till late daily 🚇 Bugis, then bus 401 (Sat, Sun, hols only)

MAXWELL ROAD (£)

This hawker centre is nicely old-fashioned – not many bright lights or modern conveniences. The food is good, especially some of the basics like chicken rice and *murtabak*.

bll; E8 ✉ Corner of Maxwell Road and South Bridge Road ⏰ Early till late daily 🚇 Tanjong Pagar

NEWTON CIRCUS (£)

Probably the most expensive of the hawker centres, and popular with bus tours. More than 100 stalls offer every type of local food. Lobster is good, and try the carrot cake (stir-fried radish with eggs).

D5 ✉ Clemenceau Avenue ⏰ Daily 24 hours 🚇 Newton

TAMAN SERASI (£)

This small hawker centre, near the Botanic Gardens, serves excellent fruit juices and *roti john*, a Malay dish like a savoury mince French bread sandwich.

A5 ✉ Cluny Road ⏰ Daily 6AM–8PM 🚇 Orchard

PICNIC FOOD COURT (£)

This air-conditioned food court in the basement of Scotts shopping centre is handy when you are shopping. A variety of stalls include Korean, Thai, Indian, Japanese, Malay, steamboat and vegetarian options.

C5 ✉ Picnic Food Court, Scotts , Scotts Road ⏰ Sun–Thu 10:30–10; Fri, Sat, eve of public hols 10:30–10:30 🚇 Orchard

ZHUJIAO FOOD CENTRE (£)

A good place to watch the world go by. Get up early and have an Indian breakfast being prepared: *roti prata* (curry gravy with bread) and, to drink, *teh tarik* (aerated tea).

E5 ✉ Zhujiao Food Market, Serangoon Road ⏰ Daily early till late 🚇 Bugis

Popular orders at a glance

Char kway teow Flat noodles with prawns, pork and beansprouts.

Beef kway teow Flat noodles with beef.

Chicken rice As it sounds!

Laksa Rice noodles and prawns in coconut milk with chilli.

Mee goreng Fried spicy noodles.

Nasi biryani Rice and spiced chicken or mutton.

Shabu-shabu The name refers to the sound made as paper-thin beef is moved back and forth in a bubbling broth. It is cooked at the table in a copper pot.

Murtabak Pancake with minced chicken, mutton or sardine filling.

Chilli crab Crab, chilli and tomato sauce, garlic; served in the shell.

Ice kacang Red beans, jelly, sweet corn, shaved ice and evaporated milk.

Bandung Rose syrup and evaporated milk – it's the lurid pink drink!

65

ITALIAN

A taste of Italy

Singaporeans and visitors alike have latched on to Italian cuisine and new Italian restaurants are springing up all the time all over Singapore. Even fast-food chains such as Pizza Hut and Milano's do well. So if you're craving something other than rice and Asian noodles, you might want to look out for fresh Italian pasta and pizzas.

AL FORNO TRATTORIA (££)

A popular restaurant, though a little way out of the centre of the city, so be sure to make a reservation. Antipasto and pizzas are particularly tasty.

🔀 D4 🖂 #01-05 Goldhill Plaza, Newton Road ☎ 256 2848 🕙 Daily 12–2, 6:30–10:30 🚇 Novena

IL PICCOLO (££)

Though small, this neighbourhood eatery is big on flavour and a good choice. A diner-style restaurant with an imaginative selection of pastas and desserts.

🔀 off map to northwest 🖂 557 Bukit Timah Road, #01-06 Crown Centre ☎ 468 5837 🕙 Tue–Sun 12–2:30, 6:30–10 🚌 Newton then bus 66, 67, 74, 151, 154, 156, 157, 170, 171, 174

LA FORKETTA (££)

A little off the beaten track, but it's worth the trip, as the food is delicious, particularly the pizza.

🔀 off map to west 🖂 491 River Valley Road ☎ 836 3373 🕙 Daily 12–2:30, 6–10:30 🚌 14, 32, 54, 65, 139, 195

PASTA BRAVA (££)

A lovely restaurant in a converted shophouse on the edge of Chinatown. Some dishes can be expensive, but the food is very good. This place is popular with workers at lunch.

🔀 bII; D8 🖂 11 Craig Road ☎ 227 7550 🕙 Daily 11–2:30, 6:30–10:30 🚇 Tanjong Pagar

PETE'S PLACE (£££)

This basement trattoria opened in 1973 is popular with both visitors and locals. The pastas are tasty and an excellent salad bar makes the place a good bet for vegetarians. Sunday brunches.

🔀 C5 🖂 Basement, Grand Hyatt Hotel, 10–12 Scotts Road ☎ 738 1234 🕙 Daily 11:30–2:30, 6–11 🚇 Orchard

PREGO (££)

This long-established restaurant bustles at lunch and in the evenings thanks to an excellent range of dishes and central location.

🔀 E7 🖂 Westin Stamford Hotel, 2 Stamford Road ☎ 431 5156 🕙 Daily 11:30–2:30, 6:30–10:30 🚇 City Hall

PRONTO (££)

An open-air restaurant next to the Oriental Hotel's fifth-floor pool. The *antipasti misto* is good. Leave room for tiramisu.

🔀 F7 🖂 The Oriental Hotel, 5 Raffles Avenue ☎ 331 0551 🕙 Daily 11–10:30 🚇 City Hall

ROCKY'S (££)

If you feel like ordering pizza for delivery, Rocky's is the place. Two branches. Allow an hour.

🔀 L5 🖂 419 East Coast Road ☎ 440 9112 🕙 Daily 11–10:30 (last order 10) 🚇 Eunos
🔀 off map to west 🖂 61 Sunset Way, Clementi Park Shopping Centre ☎ 468 9188 🕙 As above 🚇 Clementi

OTHER WESTERN FARE

BRAZIL CHURRASCARIA (££)

Possibly Singapore's only Brazilian eating place. Choose from the extensive, interesting set-price salad bar and then take as many as you like of the succulent spit-roasted cuts of meat brought to your table in rapid succession.

✚ off map to west ✉ 14/16 Sixth Avenue, just off Bukit Timah Road ☎ 463 1923 ⏰ Daily 6:30–10:30 🚇 Newton then bus 156, 170, 174

CHA CHA CHA (££)

A bright and cheerful Mexican restaurant in Holland Village. The cheese and mushroom burritos are delicious.

✚ off map to west ✉ 32 Lorong Mambong, Holland Village ☎ 462 1650 ⏰ Daily 11–11:30 🚌 61, 106

HARD ROCK CAFÉ (££)

Steaks, hamburgers and huge sandwiches are the most popular items on the menu at this chain restaurant and music venue decorated with rock memorabilia.

✚ C5 ✉ #02-01 HPL House, 50 Cuscaden Road ☎ 235 6256 ⏰ Sunday–Thursday 7.30AM–11–10:30 (for food) 🚇 Orchard

J P BASTIANI (££)

Mediterranean food – mainly Italian, Greek and Spanish – is served in plush surroundings in a restored godown on Clarke Quay. There is a cool bar downstairs.

✚ E7 ✉ #01-12 Clarke Quay ☎ 433 0156 ⏰ Daily 11:30–2:30, 6–11 🚇 City Hall 🚌 32, 54, 195

LATOUR (£££)

Singapore's finest French restaurant, in one of the city's leading hotels, is costly, but the service, food, setting and ambience are wonderful.

✚ B5 ✉ Ground Floor, Shangri-La Hotel, 22 Orange Grove Road ☎ 730 2471 ⏰ Daily noon–2:30, 6:30–10:30 daily 🚇 Orchard

MARCHÉ (£)

This popular restaurant has many stands that serve dishes from all over Europe. Choose from a wonderful variety of fresh seafood and steaks, and have them cooked on the spot. Southeast Asian favourites also served.

✚ D6 ✉ 260 Orchard Road, #01-03, The Heeren ☎ 737 6996 ⏰ Daily 11-11 🚇 Somerset

MEZZA 9 (£££)

Mezza 9 has an open kitchen with chefs working right in front of you and serving food at your table.

✚ C5 ✉ Grand Hyatt Hotel, 10/12 Scotts Road ☎ 730 7188 ⏰ Daily 12–11 🚇 Orchard

PAULANER BRÄUHAUS (££)

German theme restaurant-cum-brewery serving generous platters of sauerkraut and *wurst kartofeln*.

✚ F7 ✉ #01-01 Millenia Walk, 9 Raffles Boulevard ☎ 883 2572 ⏰ Daily 11:30–2:30, 6–10 (drinks only after 10) 🚇 City Hall

Dinner is served

For a romantic evening, far from the hustle and bustle of Orchard Road or a hawker centre, you can't beat the breezy hilltop terrace of Alkaff Mansion on Telok Blangah Green. It's a lovely spot for an aperitif, or a coffee after your meal. The restored salons, hung with huge mirrors upstairs and down, make for wonderful, old-fashioned dining rooms. Also don't miss the charming toilets. If you want to enjoy the terrace by day, stop by for the restaurant's delicious high tea.

VEGETARIAN & DO-IT-YOURSELF

What's for dessert?

While Singapore may not be known for its apple pies and cream tortes, it does have something just as tempting — tropical fruits. Here's a rundown of favourites:

Durian This huge, spiky fruit, when opened, reveals a creamy-yellow, soft, slimy interior and smells phenomenally bad. However, if you can get used to the aroma, the taste is not unpleasant. Not for the fainthearted!

Guava Looking like huge pears, guavas usually have a pink granular flesh that is used to make a thick, sweet drink.

Rambutan This small, red, hairy fruit sold in bunches is delicious. The firm, white flesh is sweet and rather like that of a lychee.

Papaya This large, elongated fruit is traditionally served for breakfast with lime juice and is rich in vitamin A.

VEGETARIAN

FUT SAI KAI VEGETARIAN RESTAURANT (££)

Few Chinese are vegetarians, but this unusual restaurant serves Buddhist cuisine. In addition to the many vegetables on the menu, tofu and soy bean products, often shaped to resemble meat or fish, are a speciality.

F5 ✉ 147 Kitchener Road ☎ 298 0336 ⏰ Daily 10–9 🚇 Bugis

LINGZHI VEGETARIAN RESTAURANT (£)

This restaurant has an eat-in area designed like a Chinese courtyard, and a busy takeaway counter. Popular dishes such as braised spinach, barbecued mushrooms and braised beancurd skin roll disappear quickly at this well-patronised restaurant. Imaginative menu.

C5 ✉ #B1-17/18 Orchard Towers, 400 Orchard Road ☎ 734 3788 ⏰ Daily 11:30–3:30, 6–10 🚇 Orchard

OLIO DOME (££)

This restaurant chain serves an exciting range of salads, foccacia bread sandwiches and other snacks. Good choices for vegetarians.

C5 ✉ Level 3, Wheelock Place, 501 Orchard Road ☎ 737 6958 ⏰ Daily 10:30–10:30 🚇 Orchard

ORIGINAL SIN (££)

The menu at this Mediterranean-style restaurant is completely vegetarian. The imaginative use of ingredients gives run-of-the-mill dishes a real twist.

➕ off map to west ✉ Block 43, Jalan Merah Saga, #01-62 Chip Bee Gardens, Holland Village ☎ 475 5605 ⏰ Tue–Sun 11–2:30, 6–10:30 🚌 5, 7, 61, 106

SRI VIJAYA (£)

Modest vegetarian banana-leaf establishment offering great value with its generous helpings of rice and vegetable accompaniments.

E6 ✉ 229 Selegie Road ☎ 336 1748 ⏰ Daily 7AM–10PM 🚇 Bugis

WANSEN PALACE VEGETARIAN (££)

This is a wonderful Chinese vegetarian restaurant tucked away on Craig Road. Try the mock prawns – they aren't real, but they can fool anyone.

➕ bill; D8 ✉ 2 Craig Road ☎ 227 7156/227 7157 ⏰ Daily 11-2.30, 5.30-9.30 🚇 Tanjong Pagar

DO-IT-YOURSELF

If you want provisions for a picnic, check out these supermarkets.

COLD STORAGE CENTREPOINT

D6 ✉ #B1-14 Centrepoint, 176 Orchard Road ☎ 737 4222 ⏰ Daily 9AM–10PM 🚇 Somerset

JASON'S SUPERMARKET

C5 ✉ 1 Claymore Drive, #01-01 Orchard Towers ☎ 235 4355 ⏰ Mon–Thu & Sat 8AM–9PM; Fri 8AM–10:30PM; Sun 9–9 🚇 Orchard

COFFEE & TEA

AH TENG'S BAKERY (££)
This café in Raffles Hotel Arcade sells breads, cakes and ice-creams. Try the giant whole grain muffins – a meal in themselves.
➕ F6 ✉ 1 Beach Road
☎ 331 1711 ⏰ Daily 7:30AM–11PM 🚇 City Hall

COFFEE CLUB, HOLLAND VILLAGE (£)
The Coffee Club specialises in interesting coffees, some with cream and a choice of different spirits.
➕ off the map to west ✉ 48 Lorong Mambong ☎ 466 0296 ⏰ Daily 10AM–11PM 🚌 5, 7, 61, 106

COMPASS ROSE RESTAURANT (££)
Every day there is a wonderful high tea here, in more senses than one – you're on the 72nd floor.
➕ F7 ✉ Westin Stamford Hotel, 2 Stamford Road
☎ 338 8585 ⏰ Daily 11:30–5:30 🚇 City Hall

DELIFRANCE (£)
One of a growing chain of cafés, this serves filled baguettes and other savouries and tempting sweets.
➕ E7 ✉ #01-03, 11 Stamford Road ☎ 334 1645 ⏰ Daily 7:30AM–10PM 🚇 City Hall

GOODWOOD PARK HOTEL (££)
Tea is served in a light and airy dining room overlooking the hotel pool. A pianist lends a musical note.
➕ C5 ✉ 22 Scotts Road
☎ 737 7411 ⏰ Daily 12:30–5:30 🚇 Orchard

HILTON HOTEL (££)
The Hilton clearly has a number of first-rate pastry chefs; the cake selection at teatime is a delight. Do not miss the special cheesecakes.
➕ C5 ✉ 581 Orchard Road
☎ 737 2233 ⏰ 12–5:30 Sat only 🚇 Orchard

RAFFLES HOTEL (££)
A sumptous tea is served in the Tiffin Room and the Bar and Billiard restaurant. Arrive early for afternoon tea, especially at weekends.
➕ F6 ✉ 1 Beach Road
☎ 337 1886 ⏰ Daily 3:30–5 🚇 City Hall

WESTERN-STYLE COFFEE OUTLETS

Singapore has many Western coffee outlets. Some of the best for people-watching are on Orchard Road.

STARBUCKS (£)
➕ C5 ✉ Orchard Point, 160 Orchard Road ☎ 738 6940 ⏰ Sun–Thur 7.30AM–11PM; Fri, Sat 7.30AM–midnight 🚇 Somerset

SPINELLI'S (£)
➕ D6 ✉ Heeren Building, Orchard Road ☎ 738 0233 ⏰ Mon–Thu 7.30AM–10PM; Fri, Sat 7.30AM–midnight; Sun 9AM–10PM 🚇 Somerset

THE COFFEE BEAN & TEA LEAF (£)
➕ C5 ✉ #01-04/05 The Promenade, Orchard Road ☎ 734 0090 ⏰ Sun–Thu 8.00AM–10.30PM; Fri, Sat 8AM–1AM 🚇 Orchard

Coffee shops

Singapore's traditional coffee shops are nothing like the modern places that sell a sophisticated selection of Javanese coffee and brownies. They are no-nonsense, cheap and cheerful options for favourite local rice and noodle dishes. You also get coffee, but it's thick and sweet, made with condensed milk. Mindful of waste, coffee shops sometimes serve takeaway coffee in empty condensed-milk cans, and you will occasionally see people carrying these, though the more usual coffee container today is the familiar Styrofoam container or a plastic bag, which you can sometimes see tied to knobs or railings while the contents cool.

D ROAD WEST

Changing times

'Beyond the bazaar, ... Orchard Road becomes a straight, well-shaded drive, leading to the European residences in the Tanglin district. On the left, almost hidden by the trees is a very large Chinese Burial Ground formerly used by the Teo Chews, ie Chinese hailing from Swatow. The visitor may perhaps overtake a funeral on its way to one of these Chinese burying grounds in the suburbs, with the customary accompaniments of gongs to startle, and the scattering of gold and silver paper to appease the spirit of the deceased. Orchard Road ends at the entrance to the Military Barracks in Tanglin Road.'

– The Revd G M Reith, *Handbook to Singapore*, 1907, OUP.

TANGLIN MALL

This shopping centre provides something a little different from the designer labels on offer elsewhere on Orchard Road. The range of stores includes some interesting children's shops, a sports shop and three floors of Food Junction. A handicrafts market is held the third Saturday of every month.

✚ B5 ✉ 163 Tanglin Road
☎ 736 4922 🕐 Daily 10–10
🚇 Orchard

TANGLIN SHOPPING CENTRE

One of the area's oldest shopping centres, this is well known for its Asian antiques and curios (though, as elsewhere in Singapore, prices are high). It is also good for carpets, tailoring and cameras and accessories. Near the intersection of Tanglin and Orchard Roads.

✚ B5 ✉ 19 Tanglin Road
☎ 737 0849 🕐 Daily 10–6
🚇 Orchard

ORCHARD TOWERS

Many small specialist traders fill this centre, known particularly for its jewellery and silk shops. There are also a number of restaurants on the upper floors.

✚ C5 ✉ 400 Orchard Road
🕐 Daily 9:30AM–10PM
🚇 Orchard

WHEELOCK PLACE

This striking and ideally located centre is very popular. A Borders bookshop takes up

much of the ground floor and is open longer hours than other shops. Marks & Spencer has the basement. There's also an organic food shop.

✚ C5 ✉ 501 Orchard Road
🕐 Sun–Thu 10:30–8:30; Fri, Sat 10:30–9:30 🚇 Orchard

SHAW CENTRE

This office-cum-small-shops centre is linked to Shaw House (see below) and has a number of interesting outlets, including a reasonably priced shoe shop (Fairlady), a small clothes shop (Solo), a number of gift shops and a hardware shop (Handyman Centre).

✚ C5 ✉ 1 Scotts Road
☎ 737 9080 🕐 Daily 10–7
🚇 Orchard

SHAW HOUSE

This is a very useful shopping centre with a supermarket and inexpensive cafés in the basement, a top-floor cinema and a well-stocked department store.

✚ C5 ✉ 350 Orchard Road
☎ 235 1150 🕐 Daily 10–10
🚇 Orchard

PACIFIC PLAZA

Pacific Plaza is another trendy place popular with Singapore youth. They seem to queue for hours to get into Venom, a nightclub in the complex. Tower Records and Books fills two floors with books, music and magazines.

✚ C5 ✉ 9 Scotts Road
☎ 733 5655 🕐 Daily 10–10
🚇 Orchard

ORCHARD ROAD EAST

FAR EAST PLAZA
More than 800 outlets offering almost everything, from clothes to haircuts, CDs and software to shoe repairs.

C5 ✉ 14 Scotts Road
☎ 734 2325 🕐 Daily 10–9
Ⓜ Orchard

SCOTTS
This relatively small centre is very good for fashion items. With the Picnic Food Court in the basement and a SISTIC (Singapore Indoor Stadium Ticketing) counter for theatre tickets, it's a handy emporium.

C5 ✉ 6 Scotts Road
☎ 734 7560 🕐 Daily 10–9
(food court 11–10) Ⓜ Orchard

TANGS
Conveniently situated above Orchard MRT, this is Singapore's most famed department store and is a useful meeting point. Good for gift shopping.

C5 ✉ 320 Orchard Road
☎ 737 5500 🕐 Mon–Fri
11–9; Sat 11–9:30; Sun
12:30–8 Ⓜ Orchard

LUCKY PLAZA
Another huge shopping complex, full of small shops selling all manner of goods. Salespeople may be aggressive, so bargain hard.

C5 ✉ 304 Orchard Road
☎ 235 3294 🕐 Daily 10–9
Ⓜ Orchard

NGEE ANN CITY (► 30)

THE HEEREN
A favourite among the hip and trendy. Browse the three floors of HMV or sip coffee at Spinelli's outdoor café.

D6 ✉ 260 Orchard Road
☎ 733 4725 🕐 Daily
10AM–11PM Ⓜ Somerset

SPECIALISTS' SHOPPING CENTRE
One of Singapore's older shopping centres, named for the doctors who have offices there. This offers a number of boutiques as well as the John Little department store and a SISTIC ticket outlet.

D6 ✉ 277 Orchard Road
☎ 737 8222 🕐 Daily
10:30–8:30 Ⓜ Somerset

CENTREPOINT
One of the most user-friendly centres, with good department stores (Robinson's and Marks & Spencer) and shops selling everything from books to clothes and electrical goods, plus restaurants and a supermarket.

D6 ✉ 176 Orchard Road
☎ 235 6629 🕐 Daily
10:30–9:30 Ⓜ Somerset

CUPPAGE TERRACE
A pleasant change from large, glitzier shopping centres, Cuppage Terrace offers a small selection of arts and crafts shops.

D6 ✉ 55 Cuppage Road
🕐 Daily 10–7 Ⓜ Somerset

PLAZA SINGAPURA
Boutiques, eateries, a few department stores and cinema.

E6 ✉ 68 Orchard Road
☎ 332 9298 🕐 Daily 11–9
Ⓜ Dhoby Ghaut

Emerald Hill Road
(D5–D6)
Originally a nutmeg plantation, Emerald Hill Road features magnificent Peranakan residences, built by wealthy Straits-born Teochew Chinese. Pronounced a preservation area in 1981, it has 112 terrace houses erected from 1902 to 1930. Despite being designed by 13 different architects, the streetscape is an aesthetic blend of richly detailed townhouses. To get there, walk up the side road through Peranakan Place on Orchard Road. The stretch just above Peranakan Place also offers a few watering holes, including a wine bar and a beer bar.

CHINATOWN & THE SINGAPORE RIVER

Bargaining

Many Singapore shopkeepers are happy for you to bargain with them and it can save you a significant percentage, even on fairly small purchases. Don't make your first offer until the seller has reduced the opening price at least once. It is considered a matter of honour that once you have settled on a price, you must go through with the deal. Don't bargain if you see 'Fixed price' signs.

Hong bao

You may notice small red packets on sale. These *hong bao*, as they are known, are used for giving gifts of money, particularly for weddings and at Chinese New Year, when it is the custom for unmarried children to receive a red packet. Many employers also choose this time of year to give their red packets – bonuses.

CLARKE QUAY & RIVERSIDE POINT (► 38)

This area is gaining a reputation as a bargain haunt with their Sunday flea market and over 80 shops selling everything from curios to designer wear. Adjacent to Clarke Quay is Liang Court and Robertson walk.

🔡 b|; E7 ✉ 3 River Valley Road ☎ 433 0152 🚇 Raffles Place

CHINATOWN POINT

One of Chinatown's earliest shopping centres, containing a variety of shops and eateries, and specialising in local handicraft and gift shops.

🔡 b||; D8 ✉ 133 New Bridge Road ☎ 534 0112 🕐 Daily 10–10 🚇 Outram Park

GREAT WORLD CITY

Top tenants in this sprawling complex include OG and Ethan Allen. A stone's throw from Orchard Road, the centre provides a free shuttle bus from Lucky Plaza and the Paragon, and there are a variety of eateries.

🔡 C6 ✉ Kim Seng Promenade ☎ 737 3855 🕐 Daily 10–10 🚌 16

PEOPLE'S PARK COMPLEX

You can buy all manner of goods at this bustling centre in the heart of Chinatown including traditional remedies and Asian textiles. There are plenty of clothing and electronic shops too This is one of the city's oldest shopping centres.

🔡 b||; D8 ✉ 1 Park Road ☎ 535 9533 🕐 Daily 10–9:30 🚇 Outram Park

PIDEMCO CENTRE

The Pidemco Centre, home of the Singapore Jewellery Mart, is a good starting point to get an overview of the range and cost of jewellery available here.

🔡 d; E7 ✉ 95 South Bridge Road ☎ 232 9392 🕐 Mon–Sat 10:30–6 🚇 City Hall

TEMPLE/PAGODA/ TRENGGANU STREETS

In the streets between South Bridge Road and New Bridge Road, in the heart of Chinatown, shops and stalls sell a tantalising range of Chinese goods: herbal remedies, porcelain, exotic fruit and gold jewellery. The rich smell of a Chinese favourite, barbecued pork, pervades the streets.

🔡 b||; E8 ✉ Temple Street off South Bridge Road 🚇 Outram Park

YUE HWA CHINESE PRODUCTS EMPORIUM

This well laid-out department store in the heart of Chinatown has an extensive array of quality merchandise, from traditional and modern clothes to handicrafts, food and household items.

🔡 b||; D8 ✉ 70 Eu Tong Sen Street ☎ 538 4222 🕐 Mon–Thu 11–9:30; Fri–Sun 11–10 🚇 Outram Park

ARAB STREET & LITTLE INDIA

ALBERT STREET
Start at the Albert Complex and work your way to Albert Court (the Selegie Road end), where two rows of renovated shophouses now contain gift shops and eateries. Sidestreets lead to still other stalls.

✚ E5   🚇 Bugis

ARAB STREET
Good handicrafts from all over Asia can be bought near the intersection of Beach Road and Arab Street, where some of the neighbourhood's original shops still survive. Look for basketware, textiles, laces, silverwork, jewellery and perfume. This is the best area in Singapore for buying fabric; numerous shops offer silks, cottons and batiks.

✚ F6   ✉ Area bounded by Jalan Sultan, Beach Road, Ophir Road and Victoria Street
🚇 Bugis

DUNLOP STREET
Bursting with colourful provisions, clothing, textiles and fancy-goods shops, Dunlop Street is a microcosm of Little India. Packets of spices and Indian soaps make interesting, lightweight gifts.

✚ E5   🚇 Bugis

LITTLE INDIA ARCADE
This stretch of old shophouses has been gentrified into a rambling shopping complex. At the gateway to Little India, it has a totally Indian feel and is worth visiting for its food court and shops, which sell textiles, traditional clothing, jewellery, Indian music CDs and tapes, ayurvedic medicines, garlands and spices.

✚ E5   ✉ 48 Serangoon Road
☎ 295 5998   🕐 Daily 9:30–9 (restaurants 9AM–11PM)
🚇 Bugis

SERANGOON PLAZA
This busy emporium is always packed with Indians, Bangladeshis and others – some tourists but many locals – buying everything from food to electrical items and cosmetics. Serangoon Plaza is particularly good for cheap everyday clothes and household items.

✚ F5   ✉ 320 Serangoon Road
☎ 296 4196   🕐 Mon–Thu 9:30–10; Fri–Sun 9:30–10:30
🚇 Bugis

SIM LIM SQUARE
(➤ 77)

ZHUJIAO MARKET (KK MARKET)
The ground floor of this busy market (known to Indian locals as Teka) is just the place for fruit and flowers. On the floor above the food sellers, you'll find a range of clothes, textiles, Indian handicrafts and luggage. The quality isn't the finest, but the market is a good place for bargains and unusual items – such as Chinese babywear. A food court is on the ground floor.

✚ HE5   ✉ Buffalo Road
🕐 Daily 10–7   🚇 Bugis

Perfumers' corner
At the North Bridge Road end of Arab Street, it is possible to buy perfumes made from a heady mixture of essences: attar of rose, sandalwood, jasmine, honeysuckle and other gorgeously aromatic ingredients. These come in beautiful glass bottles and, depending upon your blend, can be quite expensive. But the scents are very strong and a little goes a long way.

73

HANDICRAFTS & ANTIQUES

Day-old antiques

Furniture and artefacts over 100 years old, considered antiques, are sold in a plethora of antique and reproduction shops. Buy only from reputable dealers. They will give a certificate of antiquity or a detailed description along with a receipt. This proof may be required to ensure duty-free importation to the US. Prices are usually lower in the country of origin than in Singapore; they vary widely here, and bargaining is essential.

ANTIQUES OF THE ORIENT
You could spend hours browsing through this shop's fine selection of old lithographs, prints, maps and books.
B5 #02-40 Tanglin Shopping Centre, 19 Tanglin Road 734 9351 Mon–Sat 10–6; Sun 10:30–4:30 Orchard

DEMPSEY ROAD
The interesting and atmospheric old warehouses along Dempsey Road are home to a wide and fascinating range of carpet, antiques and curio dealers. You can buy everything from antique rice-carriers to Indonesian day-beds.
A5 off Holland Road opposite the Botanic Gardens Daily 10:30–6 5, 7, 61, 75, 77, 105, 106, 123, 156, 165, 174, 200

LAVANYA
Textiles, small carvings, traditional furniture and jewellery are among the offerings in this excellent speciality Indian shop.
E7 #02-11–12 Excelsior Hotel and Shopping Centre, 5 Coleman Street 339 9400 Mon–Sat 11:30–7 City Hall

LIM'S ARTS & CRAFTS
Authentic handicrafts, including linens, jewellery, pottery and silk pyjamas.
off map to west #02-01 Holland Road Shopping Centre, 211 Holland Avenue 467 1300 Mon–Sat 9:30–8:30; Sun, public hols 10:30–6:30 5, 7, 61, 106

MATA-HARI
The basketry, lacquerware and silver jewellery here originate from Thailand, Cambodia, Vietnam, Indonesia and Myanmar (Burma).
B5 #02-26 Tanglin Shopping Centre, 19 Tanglin Road 737 6068 Mon–Sun 10:30–6:30. Orchard

MUSEUM SHOP
A lovely selection of Chinese ceramics and handicrafts from Southeast and South Asia – sarongs, silver jewellery, shawls and woven baskets from Lombok.
E6 53 Armenian Street 332 3629 Tue–Sun 9:30–6:30 City Hall

POLAR ARTS OF ASIA
Treasures from all over Asia pack this shop. Plates and pots from Nepal, Myanmar and the Thai hill tribes, spears from Papua New Guinea and penis gourds are just a few eye-catching items.
C5 #02-16 Far East Shopping Centre, Orchard Road 734 2311 Mon–Sat 11–6 Orchard

SINGAPORE HANDICRAFT CENTRE
Five floors of shops in the heart of Chinatown, where you can find all manner of curios, including antique snuff bottles, carpets and calligraphic works.
bII; D8 Chinatown Point, 133 New Bridge Road Daily 10–10 Outram Park

EASTERN TRADING GOODS

ALJUNIED BROTHERS HOUSE OF BATIK
One of many good batik shops on Arab Street, Aljunied Brothers also carries ready-made dresses, sarongs, tablecloths, shirts, stuffed toys and the like in batik.
✚ F5 ✉ 91 & 95 Arab Street ☎ 293 2751 ⏰ Mon–Sat 10–6. Closed Fri 12:30–2 🚇 Bugis

BATIK CORNER
Leather, briefcases, camera cases and purses as well as batik shirts, dresses and sarongs.
✚ F6 ✉ #01-19 Golden Landmark Hotel, 390 Victoria Street ☎ 291 4467 ⏰ Mon–Sat 10–7:30; Sun 12–6.30 🚇 Bugis

EAST INDIA TRADING COMPANY
Prices on cotton tops and trousers, men's and women's, are expensive, but the quality is good and the selection wide.
✚ E6 ✉ 11 Stamford Road ☎ 336 0332 ⏰ Daily 11:30–9 🚇 City Hall

EASTERN CARPETS
Walls and floors are covered with old and new Persian and Pakistani carpets, both hand-woven and mass-produced.
✚ F6 ✉ #03-26/7 Raffles City Shopping Centre, 252 North Bridge Road ☎ 338 8135 ⏰ Daily 10:30–9:30 🚇 City Hall

MALAY VILLAGE
Located in the heart of Geylang, this collection of Malay buildings showcases local talent and houses an interesting collection of artefacts.
✚ K4 ✉ 39 Geylang Serai ☎ 748 4700 ⏰ Daily 10–10 🚇 Paya Lebar

POPPY FABRIC
All the colours of the rainbow are represented in the lovely Thai and Chinese silks in this store and others specialising in textiles along fascinating Arab Street.
✚ F5 ✉ 111 Arab Street ☎ 293 3143 ⏰ Mon–Sat 10–6:15 🚇 Bugis

RAHMATH TRADING CORPORATION
In Arab bazaar fashion, this shop is bursting with rattan and wicker items of every sort: mats, baskets, fans, magazine racks, chests and even babycarriers.
✚ F5 ✉ 25 Arab Street ☎ 298 4553 ⏰ Mon–Sat 10:30–6 🚇 Bugis

SELECT BOOK SHOP
This cosy bookshop carries Singapore's largest selection of books on Southeast Asia, with an extensive range of academic texts, travel guides and coffee-table books.
✚ B5 ✉ #03-15 Tanglin Shopping Centre, 19 Tanglin Road ☎ 732 1515 ⏰ Mon–Sat 9:30–6:30 🚇 Orchard

THANDAPANI
This traditional provisions shop specialises in spices used in Indian cooking.
✚ E5 ✉ 124 Dunlop Street ☎ 292 3163 ⏰ Daily 9–9 🚇 Bugis

Carpet auctions
Taking in a carpet auction can be a fun way to spend a Sunday. Several carpet companies hold auctions then, usually at the Hyatt, the Hilton or the Holiday Inn. Carpets are spread out for easy viewing from about 10AM until just after noon. Estimated market prices are posted and a Continental-type buffet breakfast is often free to participants. Auctions usually start about 1PM. Depending on the number of viewers and the size of their wallets, bidding proceeds at a fast pace. Expect to get 50–70 per cent off the estimated price, or at least start the bidding there.

WATCHES & JEWELLERY

Jade

The written Chinese character for jade signifies beauty, nobility and purity, and the stone is much valued by the Chinese. The value of jade lies in its colour, texture and translucency. The most common types are nephrite and jadeite, both of which are very hard and cold. Nephrite is paler; jadeite is more vivid. And green is not the only colour for jade: it comes in many hues, ranging from green to pure white and lavender.

APOLLO GOLDSMITHS
One of many shops that sells gold jewellery along Buffalo Road and Serangoon Road. Gold is sold by the gram, so any difference in cost is due to the design and work.
✚ E5 ✉ #01-08, Blk 664 Buffalo Road ☎ 296 1838 🕐 Daily 10:30–8:30 🚇 Bugis

THE HOUR GLASS
Fine watches from Switzerland, Germany and the United States in all major brands.
✚ C5 ✉ 6 Scotts Road, #01-10 Scotts ☎ 235 6527 🕐 Daily 11–8:45 🚇 Orchard

JOSI GEMS
If you're looking for quality loose gems, such as diamonds, emeralds and rubies, this shop is worth a stop.
✚ E6 ✉ #08-15 Park Mall, 9 Penang Road ☎ 338 7423 🕐 Mon–Fri 11–5; Sat 11–2:30 🚇 Dhoby Ghaut

LUCKY PLAZA
Many shops here sell freshwater pearls, including choker and bracelet sets. Many colours are available.
✚ C5 ✉ 304 Orchard Road ☎ 235 3294 🕐 Daily 10–9 🚇 Orchard

MIKIMOTO
Cultured pearls in necklaces, rings and earrings are available in this boutique shop inside Takashimaya department store. Black pearl rings are another speciality.
✚ C6 ✉ #02-04 Takashimaya, 391 Orchard Road ☎ 735 1184 🕐 Daily 10–9:30 🚇 Orchard

NASH JEWELLERY
This shop and a branch in Tanglin Shopping Centre (▶ 70) sell jewellery retail and wholesale.
✚ C5 ✉ #01-28 Orchard Towers, 400 Orchard Road ☎ 735 5328 🕐 Mon–Sat 10–7:30 Sun 2–5:30 🚇 Orchard

PIDEMCO CENTRE
A wide range of shops with both uncut stones and finished jewellery make up the Singapore Jewellery Mart.
✚ cl; E7 ✉ 95 South Bridge Road ☎ 232 9392 🕐 Mon–Sat 10:30–6 🚇 City Hall

ROLEX
Rolex watches at prices that guarantee they are the real thing.
✚ C5 ✉ #01-01 Tong Building, 302 Orchard Road ☎ 737 9033 🕐 Mon–Fri 9:15–5:15 🚇 Orchard

SINCERE WATCHES
Another authorised dealer in fine European watches. The salesmen know their stuff and offer good discounts.
✚ C6 ✉ 391 Orchard Road, 01-12 Ngee Ann City ☎ 733 0618 🕐 Daily 10:30–9 🚇 Orchard

TERESE JADE & MINERALS
Jade is a Chinese favourite. Check out the loose beads and stones – you can make your own jewellery or have it custom made on the premises.
✚ B5 ✉ #01-28 Tanglin Shopping Centre, 19 Tanglin Road ☎ 734 0379 🕐 Mon–Sat 10–6 🚇 Orchard

ELECTRICAL & ELECTRONIC GOODS

CHALLENGER SUPERSTORE
Specialises in computer-related products. Stocks a good range but can be expensive.

✚ E7 ✉ #06-00 Funan Centre, 109 North Bridge Road ☎ 336 7747 ⏰ Daily 10:30–8 Ⓜ City Hall

COURTS
Two floors are filled with appliances ranging from washing machines and dryers to clocks, stereos and cameras.

✚ off map to northwest ✉ Levels 2 & 3, Plaza Singapura, 68 Orchard Road ☎ 333 1898 ⏰ Daily 11–10 Ⓜ Dhoby Ghaut

ELECTRIC CITY
A one-stop shop in the heart of Orchard Road for everything electric. Branches islandwide.

✚ D6 ✉ #04-17 and #05-03, The Heeren, 260 Orchard Road ☎ 736 6288 ⏰ Daily 10–10 Ⓜ Somerset

FUNAN CENTRE
A huge range of computers and accessories, as well as photographic equipment, fill the shops in this busy mall.

✚ E7 ✉ 109 North Bridge Road ☎ 336 4235 ⏰ Daily 11–8 Ⓜ City Hall

MOHAMED MUSTAFA & SAMSUDDIN CO
Three floors of a wide range of goods including clothing, CDs, jewellery small appliances, stereos, luggage, clocks and cameras, usually at lower prices. One of the more popular with the locals.

✚ H4 ✉ #01-/2/3 Serangoon Plaza, 320 Serangoon Road ☎ 298 2967 ⏰ Mon–Fri 9AM–10PM; Sat–Sun 9AM–10:30PM Ⓜ 66, 67

PARIS SILK
Don't be deceived by the small size of this shop; anything from washers and dryers to cameras are on sale at reasonable prices.

✚ off map to west ✉ 15A Lorong Liput, Holland Village ☎ 466 6002 ⏰ Mon–Sat 11–8; Sun 11–4 Ⓜ 5, 7, 61, 106

PERTAMA
Specialises in household appliances, TVs and audio equipment. Branches islandwide.

✚ D6 ✉ #03-08 Centrepoint, 170 Orchard Road ☎ 732 8686 ⏰ Daily 10:30–9 Ⓜ Somerset

SIM LIM SQUARE
Several floors of shops sell a large variety of electronic goods, including appliances, computers, software, televisions. Look for the red 'Merlion' logo that indicates a 'Good Retailer' approved by the STB. And beware hasslers!

✚ E5 ✉ 1 Rochor Canal Road ☎ 336 3922 ⏰ Daily 10:30AM–11PM (individual shops' hours may vary) Ⓜ Bugis

TANGS
The third floor of this popular department store has shelf after shelf of cameras, televisions and electronic items.

✚ C5 ✉ 320 Orchard Road ☎ 737 5500 ⏰ Mon–Fri 11–9; Sat 11–9:30; Sun 12:30–8 Ⓜ Orchard

Before leaving home
Some say some that Singapore no longer carries the best prices on electronics. Before leaving home, check the prices and model numbers of the brands you are interested in order to have a point of comparison when visiting the hundreds of electronics shops here. Most items can be purchased with or without a guarantee; whether you choose to have one may affect the price. Read the guarantee carefully if you do choose one, and make sure the voltage of the item and the wiring and plug fit your requirements at home.

THEATRE, MUSIC & CINEMA

Where to find out what's on

Concerts and theatre can be very popular, particularly for weekend shows. Details of events, their venues and where to buy tickets can be found in Singapore's daily morning newspaper, the *Straits Times*, and various free publications. Tickets are obtainable from SISTIC and TicketCharge outlets at Centrepoint, Tanglin Mall, Wisma Atria, Great World City, Raffles City Shopping Centre, Takashimaya Store, Funan Centre, Junction 8 and Bugis Junction. Bookings ☎ 348 5555 and ☎ 296 2929.

A nation of film goers

Cinemas pack in film lovers all over the island. A great number of English-language films are shown, as well as some Chinese films usually with English subtitles. At weekends, it is often necessary to book in advance. Singapore's most luxurious film-viewing, with drinks brought to your seat, costs you about S$20 a ticket, about triple the normal S$7.

CHINESE OPERA

Chinese opera – known as *wayang* – is staged from time to time in theatres, and shows aimed at tourists take place regularly on Clarke Quay (➤ 38), but the best place to see it is in the street. Professional troupes, often from China, set up make-shift stages all over Singapore, especially during Chinese New Year and the festival of the Hungry Ghosts (➤ 22).

CINELEISURE ORCHARD

One of Singapore's largest cinemas complexes, it includes a video arcade, shops and a food centre.
➕ D6 ✉ 8 Grange Road ☎ 235 1155 🎫 Ticket sales: daily 10–8 🚇 Somerset

DRAMA CENTRE

A range of plays, both English and Mandarin, is performed here, sometimes by local amateur dramatic groups, of which there are a growing number in Singapore.
➕ E6 ✉ Fort Canning Road ☎ 336 0005 🚇 Dhoby Ghaut

INDIAN DANCE

Singapore's Indian population takes its dance very seriously, and local dance academies put on public performances. The exacting steps and hand gestures, the exciting rhythms and the brilliant costumes of dance forms such as *orissi* are an unusual delight and well worth checking out.

Nrityalaya Aesthetics Society
➕ E6 ✉ 155 Waterloo Street ☎ 336 6537 🚇 Bugis

Singapore Indian Fine Arts Society
➕ F4 ✉ 2A Starlight Road, off Serangoon Road ☎ 299 5925 🚌 66, 67

KALLANG THEATRE

This is Singapore's largest theatre; it is here that crowd-pulling shows such as *Cats* are staged.
➕ H6 ✉ Stadium Walk ☎ 345 8488 🚌 16

THE SUBSTATION

Modern, and often local, plays are performed within a small studio theatre, along with concerts and other events.
➕ E6 ✉ 45 Armenian Street ☎ 337 7800 🚇 City Hall

VICTORIA CONCERT HALL

Classical and other music concerts take place here, the official home of the Singapore Symphony Orchestra. The SSO, which has a growing reputation, plays Friday and Saturday for most of the year and tickets are remarkably inexpensive.
➕ dI; E7 ✉ Empress Place ☎ 337 7490 🚇 Raffles Place

VICTORIA THEATRE

Singapore's oldest theater is a venue for drama, dance and music performances. Try to catch a Singapore Dance Theatre production, by Singapore's first ballet and dance company.
➕ dI; E7 ✉ Empress Place ☎ 337 7490 🚇 Raffles Place

SPORT & LEISURE

BUONA VISTA SWIMMING COMPLEX

Handy for those staying in the Holland Village area, this complex includes a competition pool as well as teaching and wading pools.

off map to west ✉ 76 Holland Drive ☎ 778 0244 🕐 Daily 10–10 🚇 Buona Vista

CLEMENTI SWIMMING CLUB

This club has teaching, wading and competition pools.

Off map to west ✉ 520 Clementi Avenue ☎ 779 0577 🕐 Daily 8AM–9:30PM 🚇 Clementi

FARRER PARK TENNIS CENTRE

A short taxi ride to the north of Orchard Road, this 8-court complex is near a swimming centre. Book ahead.

E4 ✉ 1 Rutland Road ☎ 299 4166 🕐 Daily 7AM–10PM

KALLANG NETBALL CENTRE

This modern facility is in the grounds of the National Stadium. There are 6 courts here but you should call ahead.

H5 ✉ 52 Stadium Road ☎ 348 1291 🕐 Daily 7AM–10PM 🚇 Kallang

NATIONAL STADIUM

Check papers for details of major sporting events.

H5 ✉ Stadium Road ☎ 348 1291 🚇 Kallang

RIVER VALLEY SWIMMING COMPLEX

A near-city location makes this dual pool complex popular with visitors serious about swimming. An adjacent teaching pool is available.

E7 ✉ 1 River Valley Road ☎ 337 6275 🕐 Daily 8AM–9:30PM 🚇 City Hall

TAMPINES STADIUM ROCK CLIMBING WALL

This excellent wall is one of the few in Singapore.

Off map to east ✉ 25 Tampines Street ☎ 781 1980 🕐 Daily 7AM–10PM 🚇 Tampines

TANGLIN GOLF COURSE

Handy to Orchard Road and opposite the southern entrance to the Botanic Gardens, this 5-hole golf course is the perfect place to practise your strokes.

A5 ✉ 130E Harding Road ☎ 473 7236 🕐 Daily 7AM–7:30PM 🚌 7, 106, 123, 174

TANGLIN TENNIS CENTRE

There are 4 courts at this popular facility a short bus ride from Orchard Road next to the compact Tanglin Golf Course. Book ahead.

A5 ✉ 130E Harding Road ☎ 473 7236 🕐 Daily 7AM–10PM 🚌 7, 106, 123, 174

TOA PAYOH PETANQUE COURTS

The main centre for this Gallic pastime, with 8 specialist petanque courts.

E2 ✉ 297A Lorong 6, Toa Payoh ☎ 259 2916 🕐 Daily 7AM–10PM 🚇 Toa Payoh

Football etcetera

Singaporeans love to watch football on television, especially European competitions, although Singapore's own league has a fair local following. If there is one sport that's exclusive in the island state, it would have to be golf. It's as much an excuse to carry on business outdoors as a chance for exercise, and in the pursuit of that elusive deal, golfers stride the fairways of some of the world's most rarefied clubs. Outsiders are welcome at most, however, and they're a good place to meet the friendly locals. Tennis is also another popular sport, despite the humid equatorial climate. To keep fit and get cool at the same time swimming is tops.

BARS

One for the road

After working a 10- to 12-hour day, your average Singaporean either heads home to relax with family members; those who are young and single most likely stops at a favourite bar for a drink en route. Weekends see increased nightlife activity; clubs do a roaring trade and attract expats and locals alike, especially those in the courting mode. As in other large cities, there is a good selection of Irish pubs and October brings a quota of German-inspired beer fests. And don't leave Singapore without having a gin sling at the famous Long Bar at Raffles' Hotel (➤ 24, 53).

BONNE SANTÉ

This fancy wine bar in Chijmes courtyard is a magnet for Singapore's yuppies.

✚ E6 ✉ #01-13 Chijmes, 30 Victoria Street ☎ 338 1801 🕓 Mon–Fri 5PM–1AM; Sat–Sun 6PM–2AM 🚇 City Hall

CHANGI SAILING CLUB

Although a private club and a long way out of town, this makes a lovely, relaxing place for an evening drink and meal, which can be taken on the small balcony overlooking the beach, under the palm trees or in the comfortable bar. Non-members are admitted for a dollar Monday to Friday evenings.

✚ Off map to northeast ✉ 32 Netheravon Road ☎ 545 2876 🕓 Restaurant: daily 10–10 🚇 MRT to Tampines then bus 29

CULTURE CLUB

A riverside location, close to the city, this lively pub has an alfresco area, live music and a pool area upstairs. Belgium brews on tap as well as Guinesses and happy hours 5 to 9PM daily.

✚ d; E7 ✉ 39 Boat Quay ☎ 536 3280 🕓 Sun–Thu 5PM–1AM; Fri, Sat 5PM–3AM 🚇 Raffles Place

ICE COLD BEER

A noisy, hectic, happening place where the beers are kept on ice under the glass-topped bar.

✚ D6 ✉ 9 Emerald Hill ☎ 735 9929 🕓 Mon–Fri 5PM–2AM; Sat, Sun 5PM–3AM 🚇 Somerset

J J MAHONEY'S

Varnished deep brown furniture, green lampshades and bar counters fill three levels, and radiant stained glass windows lend a European style. On the second level, a quiet bar allows you to hold intimate conversations. The third level has karaoke facilities. Beers from Germany.

✚ bIII; D8 ✉ 58 Duxton Road, Tanjong Pagar ☎ 225 6225 🕓 Sun–Thu 5PM–2AM; Fri, Sat 5PM–3AM 🚇 Tanjong Pagar

THE LONG BAR BAR & BILLARDS ROOM

The Singapore Sling is usually high on a visitor's list of things to taste in Singapore, and the place to savour it is undoubtedly the Bar and Billiards Room and the Long Bar, both in the Raffles Hotel (➤ 24, 53), where the drink was first served.

✚ F6 ✉ Raffles Hotel Arcade ☎ 337 1886 🕓 Sun–Thu 11AM–1AM, Fri–Sat 6PM–2AM 🚇 City Hall

THE NEXT PAGE

Seating in this trendy spruced-up shophouse is on floor cushions and opium beds. It's popular with expats, and there's a pool table.

✚ D7 ✉ 15 Mohamed Sultan Road ☎ 235 6967 🕓 Daily 2PM–3AM 🚇 Dhoby Ghaut 🚌 32, 54, 195

NIGHTCLUBS

BERNIE'S BFD
With its beachy decor and casual atmosphere (there's no dress code), Bernie's is a household name in the pub and club circuit. Music-wise, its mixers and cocktails keep you in fine spirits.
☩ L6 ✉ 1000 East Coast Parkway ☎ 244 4434 🕐 Mon–Thu 4PM–2AM; Fri 4PM–3AM; Sat noon–3AM; Sun noon–2AM 🚇 Raffles Place

CHINOIS CHINOIS
Packed with locals on weekends, this Western-Chinese hybrid plays mainly Canto and Chinese music both live and DJ.
☩ D6 ✉ #01-01 Cineleisure Orchard, 8 Grange Road ☎ 850 9102 🕐 Mon–Fri 6PM–3AM; Sat, Sun 8PM–3AM 🚇 Somerset

CLUB EDEN
A hip crowd gathers in this club modelled on an underground club in New York for dancing along to the house DJ's garage and dance music. The bar pours speciality drinks such as Citrus Sins, Adam's Apples and Serpent's Bites. Dress is smart casual.
☩ D7 ✉ 25 Mohamed Sultan Road ☎ 738 0720 🕐 Daily 6PM–3AM 🚌 14, 32, 54

HARRY'S QUAYSIDE
A riverside location close to the city makes this one of Singapore's most popular places for a drink, and the crowd often spills out onto the pavement. You can catch blues on Sundays, jazz from 9:30PM, Wednesday to Saturday.
☩ dl; E7 ✉ 28 Boat Quay

☎ 538 3029 🕐 Mon–Thu 11AM–midnight; Fri, Sat 11AM–3AM; Sun 11AM–1AM 🚌 16, 31, 55

NO 5 EMERALD HILL
Locals and expats appreciate this pub for its great ambience and its antiques and scattering of cushions. Upstairs there's live acoustic music; downstairs it's Top 40, Retro and Acid Jazz.
☩ D6 ✉ 5 Emerald Hill ☎ 732 0818 🕐 Mon–Sat noon–2AM; Sat, Sun 5PM–2AM 🚇 Somerset

PAPA JOE'S
This vibrant nightspot, with a great Orchard Road location, is popular with locals and expats alike. The food is Tex-Mex with a Mediterranean twist and the mango margaritas are legendary. Great pizzas.
☩ D6 ✉ Level 2 Peranakan Place I ☎ 732 6966 🕐 Daily 5PM–3AM 🚇 Somerset

ZOUK
Founded in 1990, this is Singapore's most famous club – with good reason. Excellent in-house and guest DJs spin the discs nightly. It's is in a converted godown near the River View Hotel, next to two other good clubs, Phuture and Velvet Underground, all three expensive.
☩ C7 ✉ 17–21 Jiak Kim Street ☎ 738 2988 🕐 Daily 7PM–3AM 🚌 16

Dance Clubs
Some of the city's most popular include the following: Pleasure Dome (✉ Hotel Phoenix, 277 Orchard Road); Pop Cat (✉ 42B Pagoda Street) and Venom (✉ 12th floor, 9 Pacific Plaza, Scotts Road). All attract a young crowd. Nightclubs such as Fabrice's World Music Bar (see main text) and Zouk's (✉ 17–21 Jiak Kim Street) also have dancing into the early hours.

LUXURY HOTELS

Prices

Expect to pay to pay the following prices per person per night:

Luxury	over S$200
Mid-range	S$100–S$200
Budget	under S$100

Top of the range

One of Singapore's newest and most elegant hotels, the Ritz-Carlton Millenia (✚ F7 ✉ 7 Raffles Avenue ☎ 337 8888; fax 338 0001 Ⓜ City Hall), provides all you can imagine in luxury and comfort. With its sumptuously appointed rooms, excellent restaurants, large pool and extensive business facilities, it's ideal for buisness travellers and for tourists who can afford to splurge. A commanding position on Marina Bay provides fantastic views over the harbour and the civic centre.

FOUR SEASONS

Ideally located just behind Orchard Road with top-notch facilities, two pools, air-conditioned tennis courts and good restaurants.
✚ C5 ✉ 190 Orchard Boulevard ☎ 734 1110; fax 733 0682 Ⓜ Orchard

GOODWOOD PARK

Formerly the Teutonia Club for German expatriates, this hotel retains its charm. It is well located, close to Orchard Road, and has beautifully landscaped gardens.
✚ C5 ✉ 22 Scotts Road ☎ 737 7411; fax 732 8558 Ⓜ Orchard

MARINA MANDARIN

With a superb waterfront location in the Marina Bay this 575-room luxury hotel offers the ultimate in facilities, including a host of recreation possibilities.
✚ F7 ✉ 6 Raffles Boulevard ☎ 845 1188; fax 845 1199 Ⓜ City Hall

MARRIOTT

This Singapore landmark, formerly the Dynasty, retains its original distinctive pagoda-style roof and features a roof-top pool and business and fitness centres. Its location above Tangs department store is central.
✚ C5 ✉ 320 Orchard Road ☎ 735 5800; fax 735 9800 Ⓜ Orchard

ORIENTAL

The 21-storey Oriental is one of three luxury hotels built on reclaimed land overlooking Marina Bay. It is conveniently close to Marina Square shopping centre – good for last-minute gifts – and Suntec City, which incorporates one of the largest conference and exhibition centres in Asia and is Singapore's newest central business district.
✚ F7 ✉ 5 Raffles Avenue, Marina Square ☎ 338 0066; fax 339 9537 Ⓜ City Hall

RAFFLES

To relive the golden age of travel, stay at Raffles (► 24), Singapore's most famous hotel, first opened in 1888. All the accommodations are suites and is expensive.
✚ F6 ✉ 1 Beach Road ☎ 337 1886; fax 339 7650 Ⓜ City Hall

SHANGRI-LA

One of Singapore's finest hotels, with all the facilities you'd expect, plus magnificent gardens and a golf putting green. Food and service are first rate.
✚ B5 ✉ 22 Orange Grove Road ☎ 737 3644; fax 737 3257 Ⓜ Orchard

WESTIN STAMFORD

Reputedly the tallest hotel in the world outside the United States, this luxury hotel has every possible amenity, including 16 restaurants, a business centre, sports facilities and views.
✚ F7 ✉ 2 Stamford Road ☎ 338 8585; fax 338 2862 Ⓜ City Hall

MID-RANGE HOTELS

ALBERT COURT HOTEL
An eight-storey hotel comprising 136 rooms in a renovated shophouse near Little India with a Peranakan café and good facilities.

➕ E5 ✉ 180 Albert Street
☎ 339 3939; fax 339 3252
🚇 Bugis

DUXTON HOTEL
This classy hotel is a converted shophouse. It has one of the best French restaurants in town, which supplies excellent breakfasts (included in the room price) and dinners.

➕ D8 ✉ 83 Duxton Road
☎ 227 7678; fax 227 1232
🚇 Tanjong Pagar

EXCELSIOR HOTEL
Very well located, with Chinatown, the colonial Civic District, Boat Quay, Clarke Quay and Marina Bay all a stone's throw away. Swimming pool.

➕ E5 ✉ 3-5 Coleman Street
☎ 338 7733; fax 339 3847
🚇 City Hall

GARDEN HOTEL
This pleasant hotel is slightly off the beaten track, but represents very good value, with the facilities of a much fancier place, including a pool. Within walking distance of Orchard and Scotts roads.

➕ C4 ✉ 14 Balmoral Road
☎ 235 3344; fax 235 9730
🚇 Newton

INN ON TEMPLE
Right in the heart of Chinatown, this charming hotel has traditional Peranakan furniture in the lobby and guest rooms. Its café serves Western and Asian dishes.

➕ bll; D8 ✉ 36 Temple Street, Chinatown ☎ 221 5333; fax 225 5391 🚌 84, 166, 197

ROYAL
One of Singapore's older hotels with spacious rooms at very good rates. A five-minute walk from Novena MRT and, in the other direction, the famous Newton Circus hawker centre. Swimming pool.

➕ D4 ✉ 36 Newton Road
☎ 253 4411; fax 235 8668
🚇 Novena MRT

ROYAL PEACOCK HOTEL
Nestled in a row of converted shophouses in Chinatown's relatively low-key, red-light district, the Royal Peacock is awash with European furniture and deep carpets, and bed linens are plum and emerald green.

➕ D8 ✉ 55 Keong Saik Road
☎ 223 3522; fax 221 1770
🚇 Outram Park

TRADERS HOTEL
This is near the Botanic Gardens and Orchard Road. Family apartments have small kitchens and rooms with foldaway beds that double as meeting rooms for business travellers.

➕ B5 ✉ 1A Cuscaden Road
☎ 738 2222; fax 831 4314
🚇 Orchard

Singapore's only urban resort

Merchant Court Hotel (➕ cl; E7 ✉ 20 Merchant Road ☎ 337 2288 🚇 City Hall), on the Singapore River between Clarke Quay and Chinatown, is always a good choice. The extensive facilities include a great pool, a business centre, self-service laundry facilities and a relaxing lobby bar, known as Crossroads.

BUDGET ACCOMMODATION

Hostels and cheap stays

Singapore, unlike many Asian cities, does not have a plethora of good, cheap accommodation. Some of the places on this page charge around S$100 per night per room, and are of a good standard. There are cheaper establishments, especially around Bencoolen Street, and some dormitory-style hostels, known as 'crash pads', but the standards of cleanliness and privacy can be quite low. The STB booklet entitled *Budget Hotels* lists a number of places that charge less than S$60 per night.

BEN COOLEN
This 74-room budget hotel is near the Singapore Art Museum and Little India and not far from Orchard Road and the Marina area.
✚ E6 ✉ 47 Bencoolen Street ☎ 336 0822; fax 336 2250 🚇 Dhoby Ghaut

BROADWAY
A Serangoon Road location puts this hotel in the middle of the Little India district. Standards are high and the staff friendly. Good Indian restaurant next door.
✚ E5 ✉ 195 Serangoon Road ☎ 292 4661; fax 291 6414 🚇 Bugis

DAMENLOU
In Chinatown. Rooms are clean, with en suite facilities. Restaurant and rooftop terrace.
✚ dll; E8 ✉ 12 Ann Siang Hill ☎ 221 1900; fax 225 8500 🚇 Outram Park

LITTLE INDIA GUEST HOUSE
Facilities are basic – all rooms share a bathroom and there's no café or bar – but the location is right in the heart of Little India. Good if your budget is limited.
✚ E5 ✉ 3 Veerasamy Road ☎ 294 2866; fax 298 4866 🚇 Bugis

MAJESTIC
Refurbishment has stripped this classic backpackers' retreat of its charm, but the good facilities, warm welcome and great location on the edge of Chinatown compensate.
✚ all; D8 ✉ 31–7 Bukit Pasoh Road ☎ 222 3377; fax 223 0907 🚇 Outram Park

METROPOLE
This hotel, across the street from Raffles, is a cut above basic. The famed Imperial Herbal Restaurant (➤ 62) is here.
✚ F6 ✉ 41 Seah Street ☎ 336 3611; fax 339 3610 🚇 City Hall

METROPOLITAN YMCA
One of a number of YMCAs in Singapore, with a swimming pool. Book ahead.
✚ B4 ✉ 60 Stevens Road ☎ 737 7755; fax 235 5528 🚇 MRT to Orchard then bus 196, 190, 132, 105, 605

SAN WAH HOTEL
A very basic hotel in a traditional house. Clean rooms, low rates and handy location are draws.
✚ E6 ✉ 36 Bencoolen Street ☎ 336 2428; no fax 🚇 Dhoby Ghaut

STRAND
A budget hotel with café and en suite bathrooms.
✚ E6 ✉ 25 Bencoolen Street ☎ 338 1866; fax 338 1330 🚇 Dhoby Ghaut

YMCA INTERNATIONAL HOUSE
This YMCA, with a prime location near the start of Orchard Road, has a fitness centre, pool and a McDonalds is in the building. Reserve well in advance.
✚ E6 ✉ 1 Orchard Road ☎ 336 6000; fax 337 3140 🚇 Dhoby Ghaut

SINGAPORE
travel facts

ARRIVING & DEPARTING

Passports and visas

- Visas are not required by citizens of the EU, USA or most Commonwealth countries. Passports must be valid for six months from the date of entry into Singapore.
- Visas are required by Indian visitors who plan to stay more than 14 days.
- On arrival, tourist visas are issued for 30 days. Extensions are obtainable from the Singapore Immigration Building ✉ 10 Kallang Road ☎ 1800 391 6400, or by making a trip outside Singapore.

Vaccinations

- Vaccinations are unnecessary unless you are coming from an area infected with yellow fever or cholera.

Insurance

- Check your insurance and purchase supplementary travel coverage if need be.
- Medical charges are quite high.

Climate

- Climate is tropical with few seasonal differences.
- Year round, the temperature range is steady, from a night-time low of 24°C to a daily high of 33°C throughout the year. December and January can be slightly cooler and May to August slightly hotter.
- Rainfall is fairly constant, but peaks between November and January with the northeast monsoon. However, it rarely rains for long – usually an hour's torrential downpour at a time. During monsoon times, storms can be dramatic, with sheets of rain and intense thunder and lightning. Most occur early in the morning and in the afternoon.
- Humidity can sometimes reach nearly 100 per cent, and averages 84.4 per cent.

Safety and comfort

- Singapore is probably the safest Asian country in which to travel with low crime rates making it a good destination for women and lone travellers to visit.
- Be sure to drink plenty of water to avoid heat exhaustion.
- It is safe to drink tap water and eat from foodstalls and hawkers.

Arriving by air

- Singapore's Changi Airport is very well served by flights from all major destinations. Flights take around 13 hours from Western Europe, allow at least 20 hours for flights from the USA.
- Taxi ranks are well marked and there is rarely a queue. The fare into the city is around S$20.
- The airport bus (S$5), stops at major hotels. Buses 16, 36 travel between the airport and the city.
- You can make free telephone calls within Singapore from the customs hall.
- Useful numbers:
  Customs: Terminal 1 ☎ 542 7058/545 9497, Terminal 2 ☎ 543 0754/543 0755; Changi Airport enquiries ☎ 542 1122; Airbus ☎ 542 8297

Arriving by bus

- Air-conditioned long-distance buses come direct from Bangkok, Penang and Kuala Lumpur, and from other main towns in peninsular Malaysia. The journey takes 14 to 16 hours from Penang, 6 hours from Kuala Lumpur.
- Long-distance buses arrive and depart from the Lavender Street bus station.

- Bus 170 leaves Johor Bahru bus station regularly for Queen Street bus station in Singapore. Depending on the traffic on the causeway to Singapore, the journey from Johor Bahru takes around one hour. The Second Crossing, another causeway, links Tuas in Singapore's west with Malaysia's Johor state.
- Express service information: Singapore–Johor Bahru Express ☎ 292 8149; Singapore–Malacca Express ☎ 293 5915; Singapore–Kuala Lumpur Express ☎ 292 8254

Arriving by train

- There is one main north–south train line in Malaysia. Around four trains arrive per day in Singapore from Kuala Lumpur. Journey times vary.
- Immigration formalities occur once you've disembarked at Singapore's Keppel Road railway station, still technically in Malaysia. ☎ 222 5165.
- The Eastern and Oriental Express offers a leisurely and luxurious trip to Singapore from Bangkok (Thailand), Penang or Kuala Lumpur. ☎ 392 3500

Arriving by sea

- Most cruise ships dock at the World Trade Centre. From there, taxis and buses go to the city centre.
- Ferries travel regularly between Tanjong Belungkor (Johor) and Changi ferry terminal (Ferrylink ☎ 545 3600); to and from Tioman March to October (Auto Batam Ferries ☎ 542 7105); and between the World Trade Centre and Bintan (Auto Batam Ferries ☎ 271 4866).

Car hire

- Car hire is expensive and public transport is very good.

- If you do decide to hire a car, remember that it is very expensive to take it into Malaysia; it's much better to hire one there. An area day licence has to be bought to take a car into the central business district during the week and until mid-afternoon on Saturdays.
- Display coupons in your windscreen in car parks and designated parking places. Area day licences and books of coupons can be purchased at newsagents and garages. Steep fines are incurred for failing to display licences and coupons.
- Driving is on the left. A valid international or other recognised driving license is required.

Customs regulations

- One litre each of duty-free spirits, wine and beer can be brought into Singapore, along with a reasonable amount of personal items and gifts.
- Duty has to be paid on cigarettes, cigars and tobacco.
- A number of items are prohibited. Chewing gum tops this list along with weapons, firecrackers, drugs, pornographic and pirated material and certain publications. Video cassettes are subject to inspection, for which a fee may be charged.
- There is no limit to the amount of currency you may bring in.

Departure tax

- A departure tax of S$15 is included in the cost of your air ticket.

Goods and services tax (GST)

- If you buy goods costing S$300 or more, you may, as a visitor, be eligible to claim back the 3 per cent GST.

- Ask for and fill out a GST Claim Form in the shop. Make sure you have your passport whenever you go shopping if you are planning to claim this tax back.
- On departure from Singapore you need to produce your copy of this form, along with the goods themselves, at special counters at the airport in order to obtain your GST rebate. Allow at least 15 minutes. Enquiries ☎ 225 6238

ESSENTIAL FACTS

Backpackers

- Accommodation is generally expensive, with cheap options fairly hard to find, although budget-priced hostels offer rooms from as little as S$20–S$40 per night (► 84).
- Food is inexpensive compared with prices in Europe and the US. A meal at a hawker centre may cost as little as S$3.

Complaints

- If you wish to complain about the service, you have received you can contact the Singapore Tourist Board (see below) or the Retail Promotion Centre (☎ 458 6377).

Electricity

- Singapore operates on 220–240 volts and most sockets take British-style three-pin plugs.
- Most hotels supply adaptors.

Etiquette

- Singapore is very regulated with laws against jaywalking, spitting and littering, among other things. Fines for littering can be about S$1,000, as they can be for smoking in the wrong place.
- Smoking is prohibited on public transport, in lifts, government offices, theatres, air-conditioned restaurants and shopping centres.
- Tipping is discouraged in restaurants, hotels or taxis, though restaurants charge for service (a sales tax and an entertainment tax, which amounts to a total of around 14 per cent, often expressed on bills and receipts as "+++").
- Casual clothes are acceptable in most places, though some clubs and bars stipulate no shorts and sandals. Men and women should cover arms and legs when visiting all temples.
- In temples, mosques and other places of worship, be respectful: don't make too much noise and, in Muslim and Hindu places of worship, remove your footwear before entering.
- Most Asians consider it rude to point with your finger; use your whole hand instead.
- When dining with Muslims and Hindus, do not eat with your left hand (considered unclean); they rarely use cutlery. Be aware that Muslims do not eat pork and many Hindus do not eat beef or are vegetarian. Muslims do not eat and drink in daylight hours during Ramadan, the fasting month.
- Chopsticks are the norm in Chinese restaurants, though spoons and forks are readily available.
- Eating is a national pastime, especially for the Chinese, so don't be surprised if hardly a word is uttered once the food is served. All concentration is devoted to the matter at hand – eating!
- If you be invited to someone's home at Chinese New Year, the gift to take is oranges and never an odd number, which the Chinese consider unlucky.

Money matters

- You can change money at the airport on arrival, or at hotels, banks and money-changers, who can be found all over town (and whose rate is slightly better than that given by banks and hotels). Most major banks are in the Central Business District (CBD).
- Automatic teller machines (ATMs) are everywhere.
- The Singapore dollar and other major currencies are easily changed to the local currency in Malaysia and Indonesia.
- Brunei dollar notes have the same value as the Singapore dollar and are accepted everywhere in Singapore.

Opening hours

- Stores: usually Mon to Sat 10 to 9:30; some close earlier and others keep longer hours. Most shops are open on Sunday.
- Banks: Mon to Fri 9 to 3; Sat 10 to 12.
- Offices: usually Mon to Fri 9 to 5; some open for half a day on Saturdays and others open earlier and close later.
- Doctors' clinics: Mon to Fri 9 to 6; Sat 9 to 12.
- Many shops, restaurants and hotels take credit cards.

Places of worship

- Anglican: St Andrew's Cathedral ✉ St Andrew's Road ☎ 337 6104
- Jewish Orthodox: Synagogue ✉ Waterloo Street ☎ 336 0692
- Methodist: Wesley Methodist Church ✉ 5 Fort Canning Road ☎ 336 1433.
- Roman Catholic: Cathedral of the Good Shepherd ✉ Queen Street ☎ 337 2036
- Muslim mosques and Hindu temples are listed in the Top 25 Sights (► 23–48) and Singapore's Best (► 49–60).

Public holidays

- New Year's Day: 1 January
  Hari Raya Puasa: one day, January/February
  Chinese New Year: two days, February
  Good Friday: March/April
  Hari Raya Haji: one day, April
  Labour Day: 1 May
  Vesak Day: one day, May
  National Day: 9 August
  Diwali: November
  Christmas Day: 25 December

Singapore Tourist Board

- Predictably, the ultra-efficient Singapore Tourist Board produces plenty of free literature about the island and tours. Individual guides can be hired for specialist needs and free sightseeing tours are available for transit passengers; contact the Changi Airport lounge on arrival. The board's main office is centrally located in Orchard Spring Lane off Cuscaden Road (✉ Tourism Court, 1 Orchard Spring Lane ☎ 1800 738 3778 🕐 Mon–Fri 8:30–5, Sat 8:30–1). Information also from its office in Raffles Hotel Arcade (✉ #02-34 Raffles Hotel Arcade ☎ 1800 334 1335 🕐 8:30–7).
- Overseas tourist offices are at:
  Australia ✉ Level 11, AWA Building, 47 York Street, Sydney, NSW 2000 ☎ 02 9290 2882/8; fax 02 9290 2555 and ✉ 8th Floor, St George's Court, 16 St George's Terrace, Perth, WA 6000 ☎ 009 325 8578; fax 08 9221 3864
  Canada ✉ The Standard Life Building, 121 King Street West, Suite 1000, Toronto, Ontario M5H 3T9 ☎ 416/363 8898; fax 416/363 5752
  New Zealand ✉ 3rd floor, 43 High Street, Auckland ☎ 09 358 1191; fax 09 358 1196
  UK ✉ Carrington House, 126–30 Regent Street, London W1R 5FE ☎ 0171 437 0033; fax 0171 734 2191
  USA ✉ 590 Fifth Avenue, 12th Floor, New York, NY 10036 ☎ 212/302-4861; fax 212/302-4801 and ✉ 8484 Wilshire Boulevard, Suite 510, Beverly Hills, CA 90211 ☎ 213/852-1901; fax 213/852-0129

- Many hotels display an extensive range of tourist brochures and have tour desks with helpful staff who can offer ideas on interesting things to do during your stay.

Time

- Singapore is eight hours ahead of Greenwich Mean Time (seven hours during British Summer Time), two hours behind Australian Eastern Standard Time and 12 hours ahead of US Eastern Standard Time.

Toilets

- There are easily accessible, clean restrooms in almost every shopping and hawker centre.
- MRT stations also usually have toilets.
- It is acceptable to use toilets in hotels, even if not a guest.
- Some facilities charge 10 or 20 cents and will then provide toilet paper.
- Be prepared to use squatting toilets occasionally, though you will find most places offer a choice.

Visitors with disabilities

- Many hotels, shops and sights have facilities for those with disabilities, though getting around can sometimes be difficult.
- If you have specific queries about particular problems, contact the National Council of Social Services ☎ 336 1544

PUBLIC TRANSPORT

Bus

- Buses take exact change, though you can always give a dollar coin for a journey you know costs less.
- Bus service is numerous and frequent. Buy individual tickets on the bus (exact change only), or

use the Transitlink Farecard, mentioned above.
- Machines at the front of the bus take the card; press a button for the price of your particular journey. If you're not sure of the amount, ask the driver.
- Singapore Explorer stored-value cards are available for use on buses – S$5 for one-day and S$12 for three-day cards. These cards can be purchased at MRT stations.
- A comprehensive bus and MRT timetable, called the *Transitlink Guide*, can be purchased at newsagents for S$1.50.
- Singapore Bus Service runs a hotline ⓒ Mon–Fri 8–5:30; Sat 8–1. Tell them where you are and where you want to go. The number is ☎ 1800 287 2727

MRT

- There are two main mass rapid transit (MRT) lines, running north–south and east–west (see MRT map ➤ 93). The North-East Line is scheduled to open in 2002.
- Trains run between 6AM and midnight.
- You can buy single tickets, or use the S$7 tourist souvenir stored-value cards for a number of journeys.
- The Transitlink Farecard, also a stored-value card (minimum value S$10 plus S$2 deposit), can be used on buses as well as the MRT.
- Tickets can be purchased from machines and from ticket offices. Insert them into machines at the barriers when entering and leaving stations. Take the card with you when you are through the barrier, unless it is a single-journey ticket, in which case the machine will retain the ticket at the end of your journey.

- At the end of your stay refunds can be obtained on any amount outstanding on stored-value cards.
- Useful numbers: MRT ☎ 336 8900; MRT and bus integration ☎ 1800 779 9366

Taxi

- Taxis are easily found on Singapore's roads, though they can be more difficult to come by during rush hours (8AM to 9AM and 5PM to 7PM), just before midnight, and when it's raining.
- Shopping centres, hotels, sights and stations usually have taxi stands, and apart from these, taxis can also be hailed along the road. A taxi displaying a light at night is for hire.
- Taxis are air-conditioned and comfortable.
- Taxis charge a flat rate of S$2.40. There are surcharges for taxis hired from the airport, for fares between midnight and 6AM, for bookings made in advance, and for journeys via the business district or on motorways where electronic road-pricing schemes are operating.
- Taxi drivers sometimes may not have sufficient change to accept large notes (S$50 or higher), so carry some low value notes.
- Book in advance for important journeys, such as to the airport. Some taxi companies: Comfort ☎ 552 1111/2828 Citycab ☎ 552 2222 Tibs ☎ 481 1211

Trishaw

- Singapore's bicycle trishaws are disappearing fast, but this traditional method of transport is popular with tourists around the centre of town. Agree on a price in advance. For tours by trishaw (► 19).

MEDIA & COMMUNICATIONS

Newspapers & magazines

- The main English-language dailies are the *Straits Times*, the *Business Times* and the *New Paper*. The latter is of a tabloid nature, seen as a fun alternative to others and as a result contains very little real news.
- The *International Herald Tribune* is also available, as is a wide range of local and international magazines and publications.
- All publications are subject to strict government-controlled censorship; some foreign magazines and newspapers may be banned for periods of time if articles in them fall foul of the censorship rules.

Post offices

- Post office hours do vary, but the post office at 1 Killiney Road is open Mon–Sat 9–9; Sun 9–4:30.
- Buy stamps in small shops and hotel lobbies as well as at post offices.
- Postcards and airmail letters to all destinations cost 50 cents. Standard letter rate to EuropeUSA is S$1. Prepaid postcards and airmail letters are available.
- General delivery (poste restante) facilities are available at the post office at ✉ 71 Robinson Road ☎ 222 8899. Simply address mail 'Poste restante, Singapore'.

Radio

- There are a number of local radio stations (e.g. FM98.7, FM95) that play popular music.
- BBC World Service can be picked up on FM88.9.
- Classical music can be heard on FM92.4.

Telephones

- Phone calls within Singapore are very cheap – local calls cost 10 cents for three-minute blocks.
- Both coin- and card-operated telephones are easy to find. Most restaurants and coffee shops, as well as most shops and sights, have public phones. They can also be found at MRT stations.
- Comcentre II (☎ 734 9465 ⊙ Mon–Fri 8:30–6; Sat 8:30–4. Closed Sun, public hols) offers private telephone and fax booths for local and international calls, charging the official rates.
- Phone cards can be purchased at stores and post offices.
- Calls from some hotels are subject to a 20 per cent surcharge.
- International calls need to be prefixed by 001, followed by the country code. To call Singapore from outside use country code 65.
- Calls to Malaysia from Singapore need to be prefixed by 020, followed by the area code (Kuala Lumpur – 3, Johor – 7, Penang – 4).
- Operator to call for Singapore numbers ☎ 100; international numbers ☎ 104

Television

- There are five free-to-air Singapore TV channel – you can find programmes in English on Channel 5, Channel NewsAsia, Central, and Sportcit – and most TV sets can also receive programmes broadcast by Malaysia's TV1 and TV2 channels; some may pick up broadcasts from Indonesia. Cable television is widely available, especially on the HDB estates, and broadcasts HBO, Discovery, BBC World, CNN and Star Sports among others. Most hotels offer some cable programming, especially news and films.

EMERGENCIES

Emergency numbers

- Police ☎ 999
- Fire ☎ 995
- Ambulance ☎ 995

Embassies & consulates

- Australia ✉ 25 Napier Road ☎ 836 4100 ⊙ Mon–Fri 8:30–12:30 and 1:30–4:30
- Canada ✉ 80 Anson Road, #14-00 IBM Towers ☎ 325 3200 ⊙ Mon–Fri 8–12, 2–4
- India ✉ 31 Grange Road ☎ 737 6777 ⊙ Mon–Fri 9–11:30AM
- Indonesia ✉ 7 Chatsworth Road ☎ 737 7422 ⊙ Mon–Fri 9–4
- Ireland ✉ 177 River Valley Road, #04-18 Liang Court ☎ 339 3533 ⊙ 9:30–12:30, 2:30–4.
- Malaysia ✉ 301 Jervois Road ☎ 235 0111 ⊙ Mon–Fri 8:30–3:30
- New Zealand ✉ 391A Orchard Road, #15-06 Ngee Ann City Tower A ☎ 235 9966 ⊙ Mon–Fri 8:30–4:30
- UK ✉ 325 Tanglin Road ☎ 473 9333 ⊙ Mon–Fri 8:30–5
- USA ✉ 27 Napier Road ☎ 476 9100 ⊙ Mon–Fri 8:30–5:15

Lost property

- Police ☎ 999. Call only after checking thoroughly that the item is missing.
- For lost credit cards:
  American Express ☎ 1800 732 2244
  Diners Card ☎ 294 4222
  MasterCard ☎ 1314 542 7111
  VISA ☎ 1800 345 1345

Medical treatment

- Singapore's medical system is good by any standards. It offers a mixture of public and private treatment options. Costs – even for hospitalisation – are reasonable by Western standards, although expensive in comparison with other Southeast Asian countries.
- Many hotels offer guests a doctor-on-call service or can recommend a local doctor or

clinic for you.

- You can usually just walk into a doctor's surgery or clinic and ask for treatment.
- If you require hospital treatment, you will need to provide proof that you can pay for it.
- The best centrally-located hospitals are Mount Elizabeth (☎ 737 2666) and Gleneagles (☎ 473 7222). Both have emergency departments.
- Most medicines are available in Singapore. If you have special requirements, either bring enough with you to last for your stay or inquire about their availability before you arrive.

LANGUAGES

- Singapore has four official languages: English, Mandarin, Malay and Tamil. English is widely understood and spoken. A patois know as Singlish is often used. Nominally English, it uses words from other languages, primarily Malay. Its clipped phrases and stresses make interesting listening.
- English-language newspapers, magazines and books are widely available.
- Road signs, bus destinations and tickets all appear in English, and staff in shops, hotels and places of interest speak English.

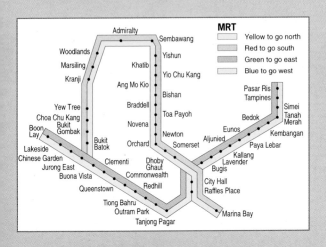

INDEX

CityPack
Singapore

Written by Vivien Lytton
Edited, designed and produced by
    AA Publishing
Maps © Automobile Associations Development Limited 1996, 1999, 2001
Fold-out map © RV Reise- und Verkehrsverlag Munich · Stuttgart
    © Cartography: GeoData

The contents of this publication are believed correct at the time of printing. Nevertheless, the publishers cannot be held responsible for any errors or omissions or for changes in the details given in this guide or for the consequences of any reliance on the information provided by the same. This does not affect your statutory rights. Assessments of attractions, hotels, restaurants and so forth are based upon the author's own personal experience and, therefore, descriptions given in this guide necessarily contain an element of subjective opinion which may not reflect the publishers' opinion or dictate a reader's own experiences on another occasion.
We have tried to ensure accuracy in this guide, but things do change and we would be grateful if readers would advise us of any inaccuracies they may encounter.

© Automobile Association Developments Limited 1996, 1999, 2001
First published 1996
Revised second edition 1999, reprinted Apr, Sep and Dec 2000
Reprinted 2001. Information verified and updated
Reprinted 2002

ISBN 0 7495 1898 7

Published by AA Publishing (a trading name of Automobile Association Developments Limited, whose registered office is Millstream, Maidenhead Road, Windsor, Berkshire SL4 5GD. Registered number 1878835).

Colour separation by Daylight Colour Art Pte Ltd, Singapore
Printed and bound by Dai Nippon Printing Co (Hong Kong) Ltd.

Acknowledgements
The author would like to thank Debbie Guthrie Haer and Tim Jaycock for their invaluable assistance with this book, and David for his support. Special thanks also to Shamira Bhanu for her help in updating this guide.
The Automobile Association would like to thank the following photographers, libraries and associations for their assistance in the preparation of this book: Rex Features Ltd 9; Night Safari 25; Vivien Crump 28; Travel Ink/Abbie Enock 44; Ritz-Carlton Millenia 50. The remaining pictures are held in the Association's own library (AA Photo Library) and were taken by Alex Kouprianoff, except for the following: page 59, by B Davies; pages 17, 49b, 52, by Paul Kenward pages 1, 13b, 18, 20, 21, 23b, 27b, 29, 30, 34a, 34b, 35a, 35b, 36, 37, 47, 53, 55, 57, 61a, 85a, by Ken Paterson; page 46, by Neil Ray; and page 58, by Rick Strange.

UPDATED EDITION *Rod Ritchie, Julia Walkden*
MANAGING EDITOR *Hilary Weston*

A01582

Titles in the CityPack series
- Amsterdam • Bangkok • Barcelona • Beijing • Berlin • Boston •
- Brussels & Bruges • Chicago • Dublin • Florence • Hong Kong • Lisbon •
- London • Los Angeles • Madrid • Melbourne • Miami • Montréal • Munich •
- New York • Paris • Prague • Rome • San Francisco • Seattle • Shanghai •
- Singapore • Sydney • Tokyo • Toronto • Venice • Vienna • Washington •